IN-LAWS/OUTLAWS

IN-LAWS/OUTLAWS

HOW TO MAKE PEACE WITH — HIS FAMILY AND YOURS —

PENNY BILOFSKY
AND FREDDA SACHAROW

A COPESTONE PRESS, INC., BOOK
VILLARD BOOKS NEW YORK 1991

 Published in the United States by Villard Books, a division of Random House, Inc., New York, and simultaneously in Canada by Random House of Canada Limited, Toronto.

Villard Books is a registered trademark of Random House, Inc.

Grateful acknowledgment is made to the following for permission to reprint previously published material: ANN LANDERS: "The Grandparent Trap" from the *Chicago Tribune*. Reprinted by permission of Ann Landers/ Creators Syndicate. THE NEW YORK TIMES COMPANY: Excerpts from "About Men" by Mell Lazarus. Copyright © 1987 by The New York Times Company. Reprinted by permission. SIMON & SCHUSTER, INC. AND STERLING LORD LITERISTIC, INC.: Excerpt from *The Fitzgeralds and the Kennedys* by Doris Kearns Goodwin. Copyright © 1987 by Doris Kearns Goodwin. Reprinted by permission of Simon & Schuster, Inc. and Sterling Lord Literistic, Inc.

Library of Congress Cataloging-in-Publication Data
Bilofsky, Penny.
In-laws, outlaws : how to make peace with his family and yours /
by Penny Bilofsky and Fredda Sacharow.
p. cm.
"A Copestone Press, Inc., Book."
ISBN 0-394-58228-4
1. Parents-in-law—United States. 2. Interpersonal relations.
I. Sacharow, Fredda. II. Title.
HQ759.8.B56 1991 306.87—dc 20 90-43446

9 8 7 6 5 4 3 2

First Edition

To Allan, for never being surprised and always being supportive. To Michele, for her boundless love. To Debby, for her unending admiration.

To Steve, for his laughter and love. To Rachel, for being Rachel.

ACKNOWLEDGMENTS

The authors wish to acknowledge and thank the following people for helping to make this book possible:

For professional guidance, Neil H. Stein, Esq.; Rabbi Gary Gans, Ph.D., Ed. Min.; Deborah Klein Batelli, A.C.S.W.; Stuart Charmé, Ph.D.; Louise Fradkin; Lucy Rose Fischer, Ph.D.; Debra Shain, M.S.S.; Paula Bohr, O.T.R.; and Diane Meadow, Ph.D.

Sherry Hoffman-Spatz, whose creativity started the ball rolling.

Emily Bestler, for expert and sensitive editing.

Carol Botwin, for foresight and guidance.

Penny Bilofsky's colleagues, clients, and workshop participants, for their input and willingness to share their personal stories. Be confident that we have protected all identities by changing names, locations, and specific features.

Friends and family members, for their support and encouragement and willingness to be flexible when schedules became overloaded.

A special acknowledgment to two world-class mothers-in-law—Goldie Bilofsky and Lillian Sacharow Heyman—who hold a special place in our hearts. And to our mothers, Rivian Hoffman and Lena Meyers Klein, who showed us the way with grace and courage.

CONTENTS

INTRODUCTION

In-laws Don't Have to Be Outlaws

I met Christine when I was pregnant for the first time. The two of us—both young wives, both expecting our first babies—became close friends as we watched our tummies grow and the days shrink until we held our babies. Christine delivered first, a beautiful boy, eight pounds seven ounces, with a thatch of glossy black hair the nurses in the hospital loved to part on the side. When I visited my friend, she proudly led me to the nursery where Ethan lay, swathed in the customary blue blanket. As we pressed our noses against the glass, Christine said quietly, but with passion, "See my wonderful son? Just think, somewhere out there—maybe she's not even born yet—there's a little girl who is going to take him away from me. I hate her already."

That event took place twenty-three years ago, and it offered me my first—but certainly not my last—glimpse into the murky and mysterious, challenging, and complex world of in-law relations. Like you, I grew up hearing all the tired old jokes:

"Hey, did you hear? I just came back from the airport. It was a pleasure trip: My mother-in-law was leaving."

"What's the definition of mixed emotions? Watching your mother-in-law back off a cliff in your brand-new Mercedes."

"My mother-in-law is so fat that when she sits around the house, she really sits around the house."

And this classic: "First cannibal: 'I really hate my mother-in-law.' Second cannibal: 'Okay, so just eat the vegetables.' "

Whoever named the common houseplant with long, razor-sharp leaves probably meant it as a joke, too. It is called "mother-in-law's tongue." There is also a Greek word that takes its place beside acrophobia (fear of heights) and claustrophobia (fear of closed in spaces). That word is "pentheraphobia": fear of your mother-in-law.

Images from movies, magazines, and television reinforce the negative stereotypes about mothers-in-law: She's cruel, she's interfering, she's possessive, she's abrasive. In one episode of the television sitcom *The Golden Girls,* for example, Sophia, the oldest member of the household, recalls the tradition of her girlhood home, Sicily: "If your mother-in-law died, we had a custom. You'd wear a hair shirt, eat dirt, and hit your head on a rock." Pause. "Anything to keep from laughing."

In real life there are famous horror stories about celebrity in-laws that have become classics. For example, Nancy Sinatra, former wife of Frank, apparently had such a problem with her mother-in-law, Dolly, that she was glad to be able to put an entire nation between them when she moved from New Jersey to California. She took along not only her children, but her five married sisters as well, according to Sinatra's biographer, Kitty Kelly, in *His Way*.

Dolly Sinatra had a reputation even before Nancy entered the picture. She was antagonistic toward anyone her son dated: "It's not you," Sinatra once explained. "It's any girl I go with. No matter who the girl is, my mother always has something to say."

Over the years the White House has had its share of in-law woes, too. This passage from *The Fitzgeralds and the Kennedys* by Doris Kearns Goodwin reveals the tensions between John Kennedy's wife, Jacqueline, and his indomitable mother, Rose:

"If Joe Kennedy became Jackie's secret ally within the family, Rose was, at first, her most open antagonist. Jackie's independent way was as hard to accept as Jack's had always been." Angered at Jackie's habit of sleeping late, Rose let it be known that participation at breakfast was expected: "Irritated with Jack's continuing messiness, Rose tended to blame Jackie instead."

Long before the Kennedys came to power, another president's wife, Eleanor Roosevelt, no emotional weakling herself, had to contend with the forceful presence of her husband Franklin's omnipresent mother. And Harry S Truman always lived with his wife Bess's mother: When Truman moved into the White House, Madge Wallace came with him. Questioned as to why he had waited so long to marry Bess, whom he wed when she was thirty-two, Truman responded dryly, "Because her mother came with her."

One of the worst celebrity in-law stories concerns Milton Berle's mother, Sarah Berlinger: "My mother never resented my going out with a girl," television's famous Uncle Miltie told Dotson Rader of *Parade* magazine in March, 1989. "But if I had more than three dates with one girl, Mama found some way to break it up. She didn't want to lose me. She didn't want me to get married. She worried how late I came home. We had adjoining rooms. It was a steel-cord story. Umbilical. Couldn't cut it."

Even when he did summon the courage to cut the cord by marrying a showgirl in 1941, Berle couldn't pull free completely. "I didn't know who to please—Joyce or my mother." Sara Berlinger died in 1954: Her son had married again the year before—

this time to a successful publicist named Ruth Cosgrove. That marriage lasted.

Berle's case is obviously extreme. Not every young bride will face a Sara Berlinger. But with all the bad press they have received, is it any wonder mothers-in-law, and potential mothers-in-law, inspire fear and anxiety in a young couple contemplating marriage? Personally, I am convinced in-law relationships have been given a bum rap. That's one of the reasons I've written this book.

Mother-in-law bashing is certainly fashionable. It always has been. After all, how many daughter-in-law jokes have you heard recently? All the blame, all the scorn, is reserved for that stereotypical witch whose very mention practically guarantees gales of laughter for any comedian. But the jokes are merely a reflection of society's skewed views. The onus is on both parties—mother-in-law *and* daughter-in-law—to make the relationship work.

I have walked into countless bookstores and found dozens of manuals telling me how to plan my walk down the aisle, how to keep the spark alive after I've been married, how to make sure my man remains faithful, how to juggle a two-career family, how to raise children while still salvaging enough time to be a loving couple. Conspicuous by their absence are the books that tell you how to get along with your in-laws, even though in-laws play a large and often crucial role in your marriage. Your in-laws are the people who have raised, shaped, and influenced your chosen mate, the people with whom he had the closest and most enduring ties before he met you.

Too often, in my years as a psychotherapist, I have seen the havoc that can be wrought in a family when there is enmity or hostility between in-laws.

Of the women and men who sit in my office sharing their pain, their confusion, and their unhappiness, about 40 percent bring stories of unfulfilling in-law relationships, stories in which their hurt and disappointment come through loud and clear. "My daughter-in-law is keeping my son from me," a well-dressed woman of fifty-two recently told me. "She won't even let him come for Christmas dinner." A thirty-seven-year-old librarian complained, "When she visits, my mother-in-law butts into every conversation I have with my husband. I'd like to love her, but she drives me crazy."

So prevalent are these complaints, so predictable, and yet so often preventable, that in order to help people cope better, I first began writing a newspaper column, and then conducting workshops around the country dealing with the intricate and complex in-law relationship. Initially, I was staggered by the turnout at these sessions; dozens of women and men would come to air their sad stories—and, less frequently, their happy ones. Thousands of women and men have attended these workshops over the past several years, often with in-laws in tow.

The workshops tend to get emotional—most discussions involving in-laws do. I see lots of anger and lots of disappointment, but mostly I see a longing on the part of most participants for an in-law relationship that is congenial, warm, and nurturing for all parties. They want a relationship that is open to dialogue, one in which all parties can negotiate differences and reach an understanding and appreciation of the others. Believe it or not, this is not an unrealistic dream. You *can* have a connection like that with an in-law.

My professional experiences have convinced me that people who have the right skills can relate more easily and more effectively with their in-laws. These skills *can* be learned.

Will all in-law relationships work? Sorry, no guarantee. As with any stranger you meet, there must be a certain affinity to make the relationship grow. What happens if you plain don't like her? It happens. Your best bet is to be patient, cordial, and mannerly. You have a loved one in common. Do it for him.

Also realize that you don't have to like everything about your mother-in-law to accept her. A relationship doesn't have to be all or nothing. There can be elements of her personality that you like, others you merely tolerate, and some you are forced to overlook. You hope she'll do the same for you.

Although your relationships with all your in-laws are vital and play an important role in your marriage, you will notice an emphasis in the following chapters on the mother-in-law/daughter-in-law bond. That's no coincidence. I believe that this relationship is crucial for all the members of an extended family. When there is a breakdown between these two women, there is no avenue for communication among other family members. No matter how far we have come in this postfeminist era, no matter that women comprise 53 percent of the work force and hold CEO-level jobs in the marketplace, a man still leaves the majority of social obligations to the women in his life. That means if his wife and mother are not in touch, there are likely to be no holiday dinners for the extended family, no birthday cards sent, no weekly calls. And if the essential relationship between mother-in-law and daughter-in-law is severed, how is the link between generations to be maintained?

This book will explore the complexities of the relationship between mother-in-law and daughter-in-law (as well as between other in-laws). It will offer a look at the causes of anger and friction that often stand between you and your in-law, and ways to prevent and overcome problems.

It is important, as you start to explore in-law relationships, to realize that they are never set in stone. Over the lifetime of a marriage, as husbands and wives grow, mature, and change, so, too, does the in-law relationship. As a young bride, you relate differently to your husband than you will years later when you become grandparents together. The same holds true for you and your in-laws. Every stage of courtship and marriage (and even divorce or widowhood) has its own particular set of challenges for in-law relationships. Certain problems are most likely to crop up at certain times in the family cycle. For example, the issue of whose family to visit for Christmas or Thanksgiving resonates most loudly in the early years of marriage, while the problems attendant on caring for an elderly and frail in-law generally crop up in the later years. Knowing what challenges you are apt to encounter at what points can help you get past them with more understanding and skill.

Chances are you will never be moved to say, "Whither thou goest, I will go, whither thou lodgest, I will lodge," as Ruth exclaims to her mother-in-law, Naomi, in the Bible. But you can forge a close and satisfying bond with your in-law, starting with the first day you meet her. . . .

IN-LAWS/OUTLAWS

CHAPTER ONE

Before the Wedding

You've met the guy of your dreams and he's asked you to be his wife. He's tall, dark, and handsome or slight, blond, and wiry. He's also something else: a member of a family. Someone else's family. And while the courtship may have been rosy and romantic as the two of you looked deeply into each other's eyes, the reality is that you're not just marrying Larry. You're also marrying Larry's mother, Larry's father, Larry's sister and brother, and probably his aunts, uncles, and cousins as well.

Suddenly, you'll be facing issues you may never have dreamed of when the relationship was just the two of you and the biggest challenge you faced was which movie to see Saturday night. You'll be grappling with the often-overwhelming question of what to call your new in-laws: Mom? Mother? Father? Pop? Mother Helen? Father Fred?

You'll also be dealing with problems that can arise over differences between your family and his: differences of religion, race, economic status, even politics. You'll be facing a whole host of expectations and needs, and learning to juggle them all. In this all-important premarital period, which can range from weeks to months, you'll be facing demanding choices as a couple—where to live, when and if to have children—while facing demanding choices as a future in-law as well: How much of a role can and should my future mother-in-law and father-in-law play in my marriage? If I allow myself to become close to this older woman, is that a sign of disloyalty to my own mother? What if she expects too much of me—can I deliver the goods? Do I want to?

Meanwhile, in any family constellation the future bride is not going through all this soul-searching alone. If you've recently had a son come home with that earth-shattering announcement for which you've been waiting for years—"Mother, Carla and I are getting married"—you know that such news often comes fraught with questions: Can I deal with the fear of losing my son? How will we absorb this new person into our family? How will I know if my expectations of seeing "the kids" once a week are realistic or not? In short, I've never been a mother-in-law before—what do I do? *Help!!*

Help is what this chapter is all about, particularly regarding that all-important first meeting and the weeks and months leading up to the altar. The road to happily-ever-after is often paved with misunderstandings and missed cues, power struggles, and petty rivalries, but it can be navigated smoothly if you learn some skills and finesse.

Early on, maybe as early as the first meeting, there are clues that signal danger ahead and a need to proceed cautiously. I call these the "premarital trouble signals," and they can pertain both to the younger and the older generations.

Premarital Trouble Signals for Daughters-in-law

1. Your future mother-in-law gushes over how perfect her son is.

   There you are at your very first meeting, and your partner's mother tells you that the sun rises and sets on her boy. He can do no wrong. Even as a child, he was brilliant, etc., etc. Watch out. This is a tip-off that you're dealing with a woman whose views are likely to be heavily weighted . . . against *you*. If her opinions of her child are so one-sided, the probability is that they will affect your relationship with her, and for the worse.

   Why? Chances are you will get blamed for many of your future husband's real or perceived faults. If her "perfect" son doesn't send his mother a birthday card, for example, or if he forgets to call her on Mother's Day, the blame is likely to be placed on *you*. It can't be him—he's perfect. Down the road she may point the finger at you if you and your husband don't produce the grandchildren she wants or if your standard of living isn't up to her expectations. This is a woman who sees things in black and white—and woe to the bride who comes between her and her son.

2. Your future mother-in-law criticizes your background or occupational choice.

   You've just sat down to your first dinner together and your fiancé's mother asks you politely what you do for a living. Her voice turns a little chilly when you respond that you're a nursery-school teacher—her son's *last* girlfriend was a brain surgeon, she lets you know frostily. Oh, and you've chosen an apartment on the west side of town? She's heard that that neighborhood has been going downhill the past couple of years. These are real signs of disrespect, a devaluing of your decision-making ability and your competence. It's not hard to see that here's a woman who will question your judgment every step of the way, allowing you little or no leeway in plotting your own course, a woman who five years down the road will look at your baby, dressed cozily and more than adequately for a summer walk in her carriage, and insist, "Don't you think she'll be too cold in that sweater?"

3. Your future mother-in-law compares you to the daughter she never had.

   She clasps you to her bosom and sighs, "Finally, the daughter I never had!" This one's tricky—don't be lulled into complacency or bowled over by flattery. It's flattering all right, but she is unwittingly setting you up. She probably has unrealistic expectations of your relationship with her, and wants more than you're willing or able to deliver. You'll always be in the position of disappointing her if you don't rise to the occasion. Incidentally, this situation can occur not only when your future mother-in-law has no daughters of her own, but also when she has had a less-than-ideal relationship with her own daughter(s). You're the second chance, the clean slate on which she can draw her vision of the "perfect" child.

4. Your future mother-in-law criticizes what you expect in a marriage partner.

   Two middle-aged women meet on a bus. The first can't stop raving: "My daughter married the most wonderful, thoughtful man," she gushes. "Every day she sleeps til noon while the maid cleans the house and the cook makes dinner. He brings her presents every night. Oh, such pleasure I get from this marriage." The second woman nods her head in appreciation. "Ah, you're so lucky. My poor son gets nothing but heartaches from the woman he married. She's so lazy, she never gets out of bed until twelve. Sits around the house and demands a maid and a cook. Never satisfied, either—she's not happy unless he brings her a gift every time he comes home from work!"

An old joke, of course, but its message is eternal. Expectations can make or break a marriage—or an in-law relationship. Every woman wants her child to be pampered. If your future mother-in-law believes that what you expect from her child is excessive, she may begin to resent you. The resentment can take the form of snide comments like, "My Alfred looks tired, I think he's working too hard." The unspoken message is: He's working too hard to provide things for *you*. Then there's the classic "Are you taking good care of John? He looks a little peaked."

Each person is coming into this relationship with expectations based on his or her own family histories. What you look for in a marriage is based in large part on your own experiences and what you saw in your parents' marriage. When these expectations are dissimilar, when upbringing has created large differences, there is a built-in danger. If your mother-in-law thinks that your view of marriage is out of line, you're in for trouble.

If you are a member of the older generation, there are also telltale signs for you to look for in a new family member.

Premarital Danger Signals for Mothers-in-Law

1. Your future daughter-in-law has low self-esteem.

   Your son's bride-to-be shows up at your first meeting in a

lovely flowered skirt and silk blouse. You compliment her on her outfit and she responds, "Oh, I wasn't sure about it, but it's the best thing I could find." You tell your future daughter-in-law, an attorney, that you've always admired women who have the gumption and the courage to get through law school, and she answers, "What I really wanted to be was a doctor, but I never thought I'd be good enough."

What you might have here is woman with a woefully poor self-image. Why is low self-esteem a marker of problems down the road? Because a woman with a poor opinion of herself is often a woman who desperately fears losing her spouse—believing deep down inside that she's not really good enough for him and that sooner or later he'll find that out. This fear can lead her to become more and more possessive in the face of a perceived threat—you. And the more threatened she is, the harder she'll work at isolating her husband from you.

2. Your future daughter-in-law has poor communication skills.

Good communication is the foundation for any stable relationship, and if you're dealing with someone deficient in these basic skills, you have several strikes against you from the start. You know you're in trouble if she avoids looking directly at you when she's addressing you; if she sets up a "triangle," making her wishes known through a third person (often your son); if she makes vague statements like "Whatever you say," or "It really doesn't matter" when you ask for a suggestion such as where to go for dinner or what movie she'd like to see that night.

Granted, these could be not only signs of poor communication skills but also of shyness or an excessive desire on her part to please. These also could be signals of low self-esteem or of an inability to assert herself even at appropriate times. Whatever the basic cause, such behavior might mean that she is not going to be willing to address differences between you or small annoyances—rather, she may let them build up, as her resentment and anger build with them. Even when an inability to take a stand on what movie she wants to see or what she'd like for dinner indicates only an excessive desire to please, this, too, shows she is a young woman who will submerge her own needs to find favor in your eyes. If she constantly dismisses her own wants and desires, she will eventually feel overlooked and unimportant, and she's going to resent *you* for making her feel that way.

3. Your future daughter-in-law sets up rigid "rules" that are non-negotiable.

   No visits on Friday nights or Saturday afternoons. You may not call more than once a week. You must telephone at least twenty-four hours in advance if you want to stop over. Rigid behavioral guidelines that your future daughter-in-law refuses to change even with gentle negotiation are signs of inflexibility and an indication that you're going to have some heavy going with her. *She* sets the rules, she's telling you—you play by these rules or you don't play at all. This inability to bend sets up barriers in any relationship; when these barriers are between in-laws, they can be a particular source of dismay. Often the son gets trapped in the middle when a desperate mother-in-law and an unbending daughter-in-law go head to head.

4. Your future daughter-in-law cuts herself off from her new family and rejects your son's earlier relationships.

   This danger sign may not show up at the first meeting, or even at the subsequent few get-togethers, but watch out if your future daughter-in-law starts making herself (and your son) unavailable for a Thanksgiving dinner, a Christmas brunch, or a Passover seder. There are bad times ahead if she won't hear of it when her fiancé wants to get together with his best friend from junior high, for example, or his buddy from the army. She's obviously a woman who is nervous about sharing the wealth with anyone—and that includes *you*.

Recognize any of these situations? If you do, don't panic. In this and the following chapters, you'll learn ways to deal with these behavior patterns and the deeper problems they reveal. With help, you may even come to respect and like your new in-law. It just takes time and a little effort.

Let's start by examining what can go wrong when future in-laws meet for the first time.

There's No Time Like the First Time

Somebody very perceptive once said that you get only one chance to make a first impression, so use it wisely. Unfortunately, not everybody does.

Carol met Robert at the hospital where he was a surgeon and she was a cardiac nurse. They had hit it off instantly, especially after discovering they were both hockey fanatics. Now they were traveling six hundred miles so that Carol could meet Robert's mother, Vera. Was she nervous? Only if not sleeping for four days and chewing off all her fingernails could be called nervous.

As their relationship had heated up, Robert had spoken to Carol affectionately about his mother, with whom he felt very close. The younger woman realized that winning over Vera right from the start would cement her relationship with the man she loved. The more she thought about the meeting, the more importance she invested it with, until it loomed larger in her mind than an Olympic trial for the decathlon.

It took Carol, a tall blonde with long hair, days to decide what to wear: She chose and discarded a hundred different outfits. Finally, she opted for what she thought was a well-cut flowered navy dress, pearls, and dark hose. She thought she looked pretty classy—right up to the minute that Vera answered the door.

As she looked Carol up and down, Vera allowed a shadow of disappointment to flicker across her face, and uttered words the young woman would never forget. "I thought you would bring home someone . . . different." Clearly, Carol was not good enough for Vera's boy.

Of course, this was an extreme reaction. Not every in-law relationship gets off to such an awkward start, but every first meeting is loaded with the potential for strife. Each participant harbors fixed expectations, with a particular agenda and with often unexpressed concerns and even fears. On the parents' side, there may be apprehension that the future in-law will not live up to their hopes and dreams for their child—hopes and dreams they've nurtured as far back as the day of that child's birth. Vera, for example, had a vision of her son's future bride as a wealthy person; a vision in direct conflict with the reality with which her son had presented her.

Parents may also suffer from an often unspoken fear of loss. They worry that the young usurper who has just materialized on the doorstep will spirit away the boy they've diapered, taught to ride a bike, sat up with at midnight with raging fevers, helped study for high school finals, and encouraged during the interminable wait for college acceptances.

For the younger generation, this first meeting generates fears of an entirely different sort. What sort of impression will I make? you wonder. Can I live up to my fiancé's image of me, or will I disappoint him in front of his family? Will his parents accept me as I am, or will I have to change to fit into my new family? Like Carol, will I be confronted with a Vera who dislikes me because she thinks I'm not good enough?

So the first meeting is an anxiety-producer all around. Ironically, one of the best ways to defuse some of the tension is simply to realize that it exists. If all parties can acknowledge—to themselves or, even better, out loud to each other with a little joke—that this situation is making *everyone's* hands clammy, some of the initial barriers will come down and you will have set the stage for easier mutual acceptance.

What can you do if you're entering this situation? Meeting on neutral ground might help—at a restaurant, maybe, or at a local park if the weather permits. This keeps any one party from having the edge from the start; no one has the advantage of being on home turf.

If the meeting takes place in your home, you can make things easier for the prospective family member by working hard to make her feel like a welcome guest, rather than an intruder. Be ready when she arrives; don't let her stew in the living room while you're fixing your hair in the bedroom. Tell her how pleased you are that she's here, and how much you've been looking forward to meeting her.

Even beforehand, it's important to make sure she gets as much information as she needs to make her feel comfortable about the meeting—where the gathering will take place, what kind of clothing she'll be expected to wear, what you'll be serving. One good way to convey the information is through your own son/daughter, with a message like: "We'll be eating at the country club. I'll be wearing a long skirt and a silk blouse, and my husband will be wearing a dark suit." Or: "We'll be barbecuing at home; I'm going to be casual in a denim skirt and a sweater." This way, your future in-law gets a clear picture of what's expected, but won't feel dictated to.

Another way to make this initial meeting as pleasant as possible is to plan it around an activity that everyone enjoys: a concert, for example, or an art show. Giving the meeting some structure and another function reduces the tension created by focusing only on how you're all going to get along and creates an instant topic of conversation.

If you're in the other seat, and are facing that all-important first meeting with your fiancé's parents, you can also do some mental preparation. First, realize that you're going to be nervous, and accept that as a given. You have a lot invested in your fiancé, and much rides on this first encounter.

Second, dress appropriately. You know that you feel best about yourself when you're comfortable with what you look like, so take the time to choose an outfit that is not only flattering, but also suitable. And don't forget a small hostess gift—flowers or candy are nice, neutral, and safe.

What if you and your fiancé are out for a ride—it's a Sunday afternoon, you've been playing Frisbee together, and you're in sweatshirts and torn blue jeans—and he suggests stopping in and meeting Mom for the first time? You have every right to pass. Tell him that you don't feel comfortable with launching such an important relationship when you're not looking your best. He'll understand—if not, remind him how he felt meeting *your* parents for the first time.

It helps, when you're psyching yourself up to meet your future in-laws, to remember that if this man you love so much wants to take you home to Mom, your relationship with him is probably on pretty solid footing already. If he weren't proud of you, he'd keep you hidden. Isn't it nicer that he wants to show you off?

Finally, don't forget that your fiancé also has a role to play in this first meeting. It's his job to brief all parties: to let his parents know you're coming and to tell them a little about you so that you're not a total surprise.

Preparation Time

Diane Carlson, a twenty-seven-year-old hospital administrator, met Craig, a middle-level manager for an insurance company, at a health-care conference in Laguna Beach, California. In the warm and sultry air, they fell deeply in love, and, after a two-week courtship, they decided to spend the rest of their lives together. On impulse, the couple decided to fly immediately to New York, where Diane and her parents lived, to share the wonderful news. Craig and Diane caught the next red-eye flight to the East Coast, grabbed a cab from Kennedy Airport, and, at nine the following morning, rang the Carlsons' bell. But when they blurted out their big news, they received a shock: Instead of greeting their announcement with shrieks of joy and excitement, the Carlsons just stood at the door looking numb and overwhelmed. Hardly the warm and congratulatory welcome Diane and Craig envisioned during the frenzied six-hour plane trip.

And little wonder. For the older couple, their daughter's news exploded like a bombshell. There was no warning, no priming, no preparation for what at the best of times is an exciting but unsettling statement. Instead, they were presented with a fait accompli: Mom, Dad, we're getting married.

As we'll see, there are a number of ways the couple might have chosen to prepare their respective parents for the upcoming nuptials. None involved dropping the bombshell at the older couple's feet and running, as Diane and Craig did.

No matter how close a family has been, parents have a tendency to feel abandoned when they hear of their child's intention to marry. In addition to the fear that the child will disappear from their lives, parents face other adjustments when a son or daughter is contemplating this monumental step.

They are reminded of their own aging as their child takes this next step in the life cycle, and they are also reminded of their child's sexuality. Although many young people are sexually active—some as early as their teens—many parents are able to close their eyes to this reality. Nineteen-year-old Beth might be sharing a bed with her boyfriend in college, but at home during school breaks they occupy separate rooms; eighteen-year-old Randall may have been sleeping with his high school sweetheart for two years, but his parents were able to deny this fact. A marriage, however, always denotes that sexual activity is going on. Parents can feel very uncomfortable when they are forced to confront this reality.

Finally, there is the very real fear that the family structure they've known for twenty years or more is going to change, irrevocably, and that they will have to adjust to an unknown, untested new constellation of people. Connie, an advertising copywriter, had this driven home to her unexpectedly recently, when she and her husband accompanied their middle daughter, Mindy, to the airport, where she would board a plane to France and a year of study abroad. With the family were Connie's other daughters, Anne and Eileen, as well as Eileen's new fiancé, Dan.

As a tearful Connie hugged Mindy in the minutes before the plane was to take off, she happened to glance up and see Dan watching her. "I was completely thunderstruck," she recalled. "I had never cried in front of him before. Then it hit me with amazing force: This is how it was going to be *from now on*—no more just me and my husband and the girls. Now there was someone new—whether I wanted him there or not. It was a shattering moment."

How can you help your parents through this experience and at the same time build a healthy foundation for their relationship with your new spouse? The answer is to do a lot of reassuring. Heavy doses of "I love you, I will always love you and I will always be your child" go a long way toward easing a parent's troubled heart.

Also, give your mother and father a chance to hear about and get to know this person with whom you're planning to build a new life. Don't expect instant love; don't expect the person you have chosen to be treated like family from day one. That's just unrealistic. Rather, let them know as much about your intended spouse as possible. If you live away from home, use the telephone or the mail to tell them of the things you all have in common—that you all like opera, perhaps, or that you share an enthusiasm for ice hockey. Highlight commonalities rather than differences; the differences shouldn't be ignored if they're there, but neither should they be the focus at this point.

Over the course of the weeks and months that you and your future spouse are getting to know each other better, there are bound to be ups and downs. These occur in any relationship. But when you write to your parents or call them, don't just give the negatives. Later, when you announce your engagement, they're liable to remember only the bad times they've heard about so frequently.

Again, once you've made your announcement, keep reassuring Mom and Dad that there's room for them as well as for your new fiancé in your life. It's not a case of either/or, as they may so strongly fear.

From One Extreme to Another

Alyson, an athletic blond tennis player, and Scott, an amateur classical guitarist, met their first week out of college on their first job as buyers for a large department store chain. Both were twenty-three and both lived at home with their families, in towns about twenty miles apart. They dated for nine months, then decided to get married. Things went extremely well at the first meeting between Alyson and Scott's mother, Gina. In fact, Alyson was crazy about her future mother-in-law. Soon, she found she couldn't get enough of the older woman's company, and sought out her opinion on what pattern china she and Scott ought to buy, what color scheme they should use for the wedding, and even what type of wedding dress she should look for.

"I love your hair," Alyson would tell Gina. "Could you get me an appointment with your hairdresser?"

Alyson's own mother, Paula, watched all this feeling like a neglected bystander. She became more and more upset, as Alyson's conversation filled with sentences that started with "Gina said . . ." "Gina believes . . ." and "Gina does it *this* way. . . ."

"I feel like I'm losing my daughter," a grieving Paula said to me. "Relax," I was able to reassure this anxious and troubled mother with certainty. "She'll be back."

What Paula was seeing was almost classic. It is very, very common for young adults, trying desperately to establish their own identity, to reject their mothers—indeed, their entire family and its lifestyle. This happens especially if the young person has had no opportunity to live on his or her own and earn a sense of independence.

Frequently, a young woman on the brink of marriage looks upon her future mother-in-law as a surrogate mother or a mentor, someone to help with that all-important process of separation, to help her develop a lifestyle that she sees as totally different from the one she is leaving behind. It's at this stage that you, like Alyson, might see your fiancé's mother as glittering, glamorous, exciting, and sophisticated—everything your own mother isn't. You may long to dress like her, adopt her customs, or serve the types of foods she serves. It's a natural reaction, but it is important to remember that it can also be somewhat threatening to your own parents, especially your mother.

If you're the mother seeing this happen, I can offer comfort based on hard evidence. Comes the wedding, and most young women begin to reconnect with their own mothers—often to the extent of writing off their mothers-in-law entirely. Experts such as Dr. Lucy Rose Fischer, research scientist at the Wilder Research Center in St. Paul, Minnesota, have documented that when a daughter marries, she begins to pull back toward her mother—a process that is marked even more strongly when the young woman begins to have children. She begins to value anew her mother's lifestyle, and to adopt it as her own. Because her need for separation has been met, she can now comfortably incorporate aspects of her own family's life with her in-laws' lives.

At this stage you may once more find yourself turning to your mother for advice, calling her every day and depending on her, without feeling that your identity as a separate adult is being threatened. You may even find yourself totally rejecting your mother-in-law and everything she stands for. You've gone from one extreme to another, and now it's your husband's mother who finds herself left out in the cold, an outsider looking in. This, too, is classic; how often I've heard mothers of sons lament, "Before the wedding she called me every day. Now, she won't give me the time of day. What went wrong?"

Patience, I urge. Wait this out. In more cases than not, the pendulum swings the other way and comes to rest somewhere in the middle. How can you insure that this will happen? If you're the future mother-in-law, early on you can avoid falling into the trap of siding with your future daughter-in-law against her mother. If you agree with her when she criticizes her family, you run the risk that down the road, when she has reestablished stronger ties with her family, she will see you as meddling and critical. Resist judging her mother as harsh, unfeeling, or uninvolved. Rather, if you see that your future daughter-in-law is shutting members of her own family out, encourage her to include them in all aspects of wedding planning.

Also, try to support her relationship with her mother every opportunity you can, gently pointing out that some decisions—the choice of a wedding gown, for example, or who should sit at the head table, are matters best kept between mother and daughter. The younger woman may be bewildered and resentful at first, but the more you encourage her to maintain ties with her mother, the more she will respect you and the closer she will feel to you later, when the process has begun to reverse itself.

Recognize, too, that your son's fiancé may not even realize that this process is going on. It's often up to you to tell her to be sensitive to her own family and to appreciate its own unique strengths and what it has to offer. Gently, you can lead her to understand that she doesn't need to reject everything her family has to offer to be her own person and that she can eventually integrate the best qualities of both families.

If this sticky situation is negotiated well from the beginning, it goes a long way toward assuring a good and solid relationship between mother-in-law and daughter-in-law down the line.

When Parents Meet Parents

If your parents and his have not met before, the formal announcement of the engagement often precipitates the initial face-to-face meeting of the older generation. Although cultural tradition holds that the bride's parents usually invite the groom's to this get-together, in today's climate, anyone can take the first step. What really matters is that this is a time for both sets of parents to take stock and size up the other family.

The unique aspect of this meeting is that the two sets of parents have no formal relationship recognized by law, by religious rite, or by many languages. They have no blood ties; indeed, in the English tongue there is no one word that defines or describes their relations. Some languages do accommodate this relationship: The term in Greek is *symbertheri*; in Korean it is *sadun*, and in Yiddish it is *machetunim*. Defining a relationship verbally is one way we begin to understand it—and the fact that there is no term for this particular relationship in English speaks volumes as to why it can sometimes be so difficult for all the parties in this foursome to relate to each other comfortably and with ease.

You, as the engaged couple, have to realize that it's human nature for there to be some jockeying for power here as your parents meet each other for the first time—and as the relationship develops over the next few weeks, months, and years. Who's going to host the engagement party? Who's going to decide if there will be a summer wedding or a winter wedding? Who's going to have a say in where the newlyweds live? These are the issues that are likely to foment competition. The real battle, though, going deeper than any of these issues, is: Who's in control here?

Now, at this first meeting of your parents, is the time for you, the young couple, to gently but firmly defuse these power struggles by establishing yourselves as the decision-makers. Taking charge politely can eliminate conflict right from the start. "Mom, Dad," each of you can say to your respective parents, "we love you both—we want all of you to be happy—and we've decided we'd like a June wedding in the chapel at school." It's *your* engagement, *your* wedding, ultimately *your* life. The sooner you let both sets of parents know and understand this, the better for all involved.

If you are the mother or father or an engaged child, it's only natural to be filled with conflicting emotions: excitement over the upcoming wedding, anxiety over your child's choice of a mate, fear that you are losing your "little boy" or "little girl." It's so easy to fall into the trap of hanging on to that child with all you've got. All too often, this struggle takes the form of trying to control your child and his/her future mate—dictating when the wedding should be held, where it should be held, whether it should be held at all.

Now is the time for all four parents to be aware that *this is not your wedding, it's your children's*. Decision-making belongs to them. Your job is to be supportive, while encouraging them to stand on their own. If the two sets of parents find themselves battling—one family wants to host a large and lavish engagement party, for example, and the other thinks such parties are just a ploy for gifts—let the couple decide which way to go. Again, it's their wedding.

Competition between the parents can also arise early on in the relationship, with each set trying to outdo the other in terms of gifts and attention. *His* parents are giving you a car for a wedding present? Very well, *we'll* give you a trip to Europe. What's really happening here is that both mothers and fathers are competing for the love of the younger couple—a contest that can really have no winners. Problems start when you lose sight of what the couple needs and get caught up in a "bidding war." Your offer of a vacation in the Bahamas is meaningless if the couple can't afford to buy furniture or has trouble putting food on the table between paychecks.

What can you do if you're embroiled in this type of situation? If you are the younger generation, you can go out of your way to reassure your parents that you will still love them after you get married, and that their presents are appreciated but not a prerequisite for this love. "The set of antique crystal stemware is lovely, Mom and Dad," you could say, "and if you're giving it to me because you're afraid we're going to love Sam's parents more than you, you don't have to worry. We will love you, always, just for being you."

What can members of the older generation do to defuse this competition? First of all, make sure you don't complain to your child about his or her future in-laws. This is a sure way to create animosity between the young people—and inadvertently to increase the competition itself.

Second, don't get into "mindreading," or trying to second-guess your child's parents-in-law. Walt's parents wanted to buy his fiancé, Faith, a lovely pearl necklace as an engagement gift, but hesitated because they were afraid such a gift would put Faith's parents under tremendous pressure to reciprocate in kind with a gift to Walt. Stymied, they did nothing, when in reality such a thoughtful and loving present would have meant a lot to Faith. In the final analysis, it's not your responsibility to guess how the other set of parents will react.

Finally, don't change your way of thinking to accommodate your child. If your tastes are simple and your son comes home wanting you to buy a crystal chandelier because his future in-laws have one in *their* dining room, don't get caught up in one-upmanship. Don't try to be what you're not.

Differences Between Families

One very real source of conflict from the very beginning of a relationship can be differences between your own family and your fiancé's. Michael, a dynamic political-science teacher in an East Coast high school, had fallen in love with Barbara, an articulate guidance counselor at the same school. The wedding was planned for spring. Most of Michael's family shared his delight with his outgoing, red-haired fiancée. But Michael's mother, Ruth, was cold and reserved. She came to me troubled. "Barbara has no class," she confided. "Their marriage will be a disaster." She felt this way despite the fact that Barbara was a member of a highly respected profession.

Ruth's problem with her future daughter-in-law stemmed from what she felt was a difference in social class. Ruth came from an old Germanic family whose members were diamond merchants, much revered back in Europe. They were aristocratic in outlook, and Ruth clung to this caste system. She was measuring her family against Barbara's: The young woman came from a hard-working middle-class background. Her father was an insurance salesman, her mother was a social worker. Decent, solid folks, but hardly royalty. Ruth felt her son was marrying beneath him.

In treatment, I helped Ruth talk about how she perceived herself and how threatened she felt by anyone who was different from her. She soon came to realize that her strong sense of self would not change because of her son's choice of a marriage partner; that his choice was not a slap in the face to her, and that Barbara was an individual with good and bad traits rather than just a person who didn't fit into Ruth's social orbit.

When Ruth's perception of her future daughter-in-law changed, so did her need to criticize. Her verbal attacks on the younger woman soon grew less venomous and less frequent. With that source of conflict out of the way, Ruth and Barbara's relationship became friendlier and more cordial.

When the Gap Is Even Wider

Problems stemming from differences can exist even when two families are in relatively similar circumstances—same religion, same race, roughly the same income. How much greater the potential for strife when racial and religious differences are introduced into the equation.

In the classic film *Guess Who's Coming to Dinner*, both sets of parents—white and black—reacted with shock at the news that their children were going to marry. Despite their liberal view of life, the white parents, played by Katharine Hepburn and Spencer Tracy, felt as bewildered and baffled as Sidney Poitier's screen family. Such a situation calls into question a family's values and beliefs, in effect testing all those involved to rise—or sink—to the occasion.

An interfaith or interracial marriage can pose a real threat to the identity of everyone involved. The struggle inherent in such a match can pit family against family, each trying desperately to hold on to or protect its own group identity in the face of an invasion from the outside. As with any group perceiving a threat from without, the natural tendency is to retreat behind the barricades and pull out all the ammunition.

Threatened parents might resort to subtle (or not so subtle) barbed comments aimed at a child's future spouse: "*Our* kind of people wouldn't wear such a low-cut dress." "I don't suppose *you* would appreciate this crystal vase. It's a family heirloom, you know." Often the weapon of choice is a completely different one: digging in the feet and clinging more obsessively than ever to the heritage that is being threatened. The Jewish father whose daughter is engaged to a Presbyterian man, for example, might insist that she attend regular Sabbath services or keep a strictly kosher home—practices the family has not adhered to for generations. The African-American woman whose son is engaged to a white woman might insist on talking over and over to her son about their rich ethnic heritage.

Linda, a lively brunette of Greek-Orthodox background, fell in love with Will, oldest son of a Roman Catholic family. Just after they announced their engagement, her future in-laws, the Kerrs, invited her to spend Christmas at their house.

"Will told me that he and his mother, father, sisters, and grandfather had the tradition of sitting around the table and singing carols after dinner. It sounded like a lovely custom, and I was looking forward to it," Linda recalled.

On that particular Christmas Eve, however, the singing of carols led to an hour of devotional prayer at the table, after which Will's family insisted that they all attend midnight mass. Will had not prepared her for this. He'd told her his family had never been to midnight mass before, and in fact attended services very rarely. Slowly, Linda began to realize that she was the catalyst behind this newfound fervor and devotion.

"What was so weird was that Will had said that their observance before had always involved just a few songs. He was embarrassed that his parents were making such a big deal of the difference between us," Linda said.

Confronting the Reality

How do you handle it when real, seemingly insurmountable differences exist? To begin with, you must acknowledge that the differences are there. Don't deny that social, cultural, educational, and other gaps exist. Denial leads to simmering anger covered by a veneer of hypocrisy.

For all parents thrown into a tailspin by an upcoming interfaith or interracial marriage, realizing that this is a time of potential tension and discord is another important step toward coming to grips with the situation. It's never an easy time, but there are some techniques that can make things more comfortable all around.

1. Make an honest list of the newcomer's attributes, both good and bad.

   Be sure to be very specific. Don't include race or religion as either a pro or con. The list a future mother-in-law draws up on her son's fiancée, for example, might include: (a) She treats my son with love and respect. (b) She has shown willingness to spend time with my family. (c) She had the perseverance and the intelligence to work for her degree in interior design. (d) She is warm and outgoing. (e) She loves children. (f) She hates animals. (g) She's always late for dinner.

   A list like this can help you separate real gripes from those that stem from race, religion, or social class. It can also help you see that a person is many things, not just the color of his skin or the cross or the star of David she wears on a chain, or the kind of job her parents have.
2. Talk over concerns with a close friend.

   Seek out a friend you know to be objective to help put the situation into perspective: Am I making too much of the fact that my family celebrates the Sabbath on Sunday and my daughter's fiancé celebrates on Saturday? Will my world *really* come to an end if my Hispanic son marries an Anglo woman? Friends can serve as a helpful sounding board, sometimes echoing back to you concerns that sound pretty silly or insubstantial when repeated.

3. Learn more about your future in-law's culture, religion, or heritage.

   Exploring the rich traditions of another faith or race can be rewarding, and can also help form a bond between the generations. Try participating in a social activity that incorporates important aspects of your new in-law's tradition; you may be captivated by the drama and warmth of a Passover seder given by your future son-in-law's parents, or the majesty of midnight mass at your future daughter-in-law's church.

The future bride and groom, too, can take positive steps to make this initial stage as pleasant as possible, even in the face of seemingly insurmountable obstacles. If you're entering into a marriage like this, here are some things you might try to smooth the way:

1. Tune in to the fact that a cultural gap may exist.

   One of your biggest challenges here may simply be recognizing that there *is* a chasm. A difference in color or creed is fairly obvious; less so are differences in economic backgrounds or political leanings—which can also be sources of tension. Your future in-laws may not come right out and discuss the chasm; one of your first clues may be an unexplained coolness and hostility on their part. Now is a perfect time to call on your fiancé to do some digging; he may be able to pinpoint potential problems simply by speaking openly to his parents.

2. Help educate your future in-laws about your background.
   The goal here—and both parties must understand this clearly—is not to convert them to your religion or anything else, but to foster understanding. You're looking for your new in-laws to understand (and, with luck, appreciate) you both as an individual and as a member of a group. Understanding begins with knowledge, so the more you can teach—gently, without preaching—the better the chances are that your fiancé's parents will be won over and even come to appreciate and respect you.
3. Don't fall into the trap of rejecting your identity so that you can be accepted by your future in-laws.
   Trying to hide or change what you really are is painful and stress-inducing at best; at worst, it will build a wall of resentment between you and your new family that will grow higher and more impenetrable every year. Such an approach would also make your own parents and siblings feel rejected and resentful. Instead, be proud of your heritage. If you as the daughter-in-law come to a gracious acceptance of your differences, it gives your future in-laws a wonderful model to follow.

Trouble Sharing Love

Even when differences are minimal and the first meeting comes off smoothly, all members of a new family enter the situation with sets of preconceived ideas and emotions. Your ability to form close relations depends to a large degree on early childhood experiences. When you feel that you have received your fair share of love, comfort, warmth, and nurturing as a youngster, you will have a good sense of self-esteem. Feeling good about yourself makes it easier to blend into a new family.

The psychologically healthy mother-in-law with a supportive family background is willing to "share" her son generously, without fear that he'll be snatched away by his new wife. She's able to surrender control of her son's life graciously and without reservation.

The psychologically healthy daughter-in-law is able to hear advice from her new husband's mother without feeling that the older woman is intruding on her freedom and individuality. She is eager to spend time with her new family without fear that her husband will be engulfed by them or enticed away from her.

An early experience that left you feeling unloved or abandoned, however, can leave you open to less generous emotions, as in the case of Marcy.

Marcy, who's quiet and reserved, met Patrick in law school in California; now, they are both doing clerkships in Dallas. Patrick, tall and rangy with a wry sense of humor, has a close relationship with his family back home, especially with his mother, Antoinette. Patrick has always loved bringing friends home—all of his pals enjoy spending time at his house, joking and chatting with Antoinette. There are always homemade cookies on the table and a ready and willing ear to listen to gripes about homework, unfair teachers, and unfaithful steadies.

Marcy, on the other hand, has lived only with a cool and reserved mother who doesn't show affection easily. Her father, whom she adored, died when she was six. Now, engaged to be married to Patrick, Marcy is reluctant to allow him to be with his family. When Patrick's folks visit from California, Marcy includes herself in any activity his family has planned for him, and maneuvers things so that Antoinette gets no time alone with her son. Even when the older woman calls from home just to talk, the person she winds up talking to is . . . Marcy. And when the young couple comes home to Sacramento to visit, Marcy's mother expects them to stay with her. So they wind up spending very little time—if any—with Patrick's mom and dad.

Antoinette's most recent trip to Dallas left her in tears. "No matter how hard I tried, I couldn't get Patrick alone for a second," she said bitterly. "Marcy did everything in her power to sabotage any attempts we made to visit with our son. What is the matter with her, anyway?"

After a little bit of probing, I learned something about Marcy's family history, and things became clearer to me . . . and to Antoinette. What was very likely the matter, I pointed out to her gently, was Marcy's history of "abandonment" by the father who died when she was so young, and her feeling of being kept at arm's length by an emotionally cool mother. Was it any wonder that Marcy, who had not got nearly enough love and attention as a young child, was fiercely protective of the love and attention she was getting now as a young woman?

With time, Antoinette began to realize that Marcy's clinging to Patrick and her unwillingness to "share" him had nothing to do with anything Antoinette had said or done, and everything to do with Marcy's own loss earlier in life. Recognizing this helped Antoinette to better understand her future in-law and to make allowances for her behavior.

What can you learn from Antoinette and Marcy? Above all, not to jump to the conclusion that an in-law who blocks your relationship with your child is acting that way because she dislikes you. It may be her own psychological problem. You should try to find out something about her background; once you have this information, you should try objectively to evaluate what if any early family dynamics are behind the behavior that is bothering you.

How can you find out about her background? Keep your ears and eyes open at family gatherings, listening to stories that are told and retold and observing her interactions with other family members and friends. Ask questions about when she was a child. People love to talk about themselves; given half a chance, she's likely to open up and offer clues about what makes her tick.

A daughter-in-law can learn to evaluate her own behavior, also. Look at what you are doing and try to figure out if its origin is in your childhood. Remind yourself that this new relationship you are entering does not have to be a repeat of ones you knew in childhood, that your future husband and his family are not going to replicate the experiences of your youth. If your father abandoned you when you were three, don't project the same callousness or insensitivity onto your husband. Your new family will not necessarily abandon you, smother you, dominate you, ignore you, or criticize you as someone in your birth family once might have. Accepting this reality will allow you to spend more time with your new husband's family members without fearing that they pose a threat to your security or well-being.

Do recognize at the same time, though, that your mother-in-law might approach the new relationship with the same range of fears stemming from her own experiences and anxieties. This may effect how she relates to you, a situation Dolores faced.

Dolores and Jim had known each other since they were teenagers: She was fourteen, he was two years older when they met. They were constantly in and out of each other's houses. Dolores, who is as friendly as an eager puppy, loved the relationship she had with Jim's mother, Louise. They would bake cookies together in the warm and cheery kitchen, Louise would let Dolores baby-sit for Jim's kid brother, Bobby, and the two "ladies" would chat for hours about clothes, movies, and their favorite soap-opera characters. Louise was as comfortable in Jim's house as she was in her own.

All that changed when Dolores turned eighteen. Now, she was no longer Dolores the kid next door and Jim's girlfriend. Now, she was Dolores the threat: sexually attractive, and the siren who would steal Jim away from Louise.

"She was cool and distant, and tried to do everything she could to sabotage our relationship," a bewildered Dolores remembers.

"She would invite Jim to do things with the family, and totally exclude me. When I came over to watch Bobby, she didn't want to have anything to do with me. No more baking cookies—she was always 'too busy.' It hurt."

Things came to a head the day Dolores graduated from high school, the day she had dreamed of for years. Jim and his mother had been invited to the graduation ceremony, of course, and to the party Dolores's family was throwing afterward at a nearby restaurant. Louise responded to the most important day of Dolores's life by inviting her son on a trip to Aruba with her starting the same day Dolores was to march down the aisle of the high school auditorium and collect her diploma.

"He went to Aruba, all right," recalls Dolores, now a secretary in a Manhattan accounting office. "I can't tell you how upset I was. I almost freaked out."

Dolores's pain comes through in her voice nearly ten years later as she remembers her hurt feelings and her anger toward the woman who soon became her mother-in-law. Although Jim, now a carpenter, proposed to her almost immediately after he returned from that ill-fated trip, and the couple was married early the following summer, the pain, the anger, and the hurt are still there.

Dolores was up against one of the most common—and the most frustrating—in-law situations: the parent who is reluctant to "give up" his or her child. He may have graduated magna cum laude from Yale Law School; he may make life-and-death decisions every day in the operating room or on the battlefield; he may be the chief executive officer of a Fortune 500 company; she may run a big-city newspaper. It doesn't matter. He or she is still "the baby." Conflict arises when that "baby" has the nerve to take a wife or husband, and loosen the ties to the family of origin. But he's still my son, a mother will wail—if only to herself.

This very common emotion is directly related to the fear of

abandonment or fear of rejection. At bottom, it's the specter of being left alone by someone you love and in whom you have a lot invested.

A fear of loss like this often can be traced to previous experiences—the death of a loved one, or rejection by someone you cherish, such as a mother or father. Unfortunately, most of us don't recognize that we're experiencing an old fear—or that it's forcing us into undesirable behavior in the present.

It often helps, in these cases, to do a "reality check" by challenging a belief to see if it holds water. Ask yourself, for example, "If my son goes out with Heather, and they fall in love and decide to get married, does that mean he won't love me anymore? Will he stop being my son?" More often than not, staring a scary thought in the face is enough to rob it of its power over you.

What if you're the target of hostile behavior that's been triggered by an unfounded fear of loss on the part of your future mother-in-law? It often helps to have a chat with her, pointing out how important it is to you to maintain the warmth and the love you see between her and her son. "I feel lucky to be marrying into a family that is so close, who loves Brad so much and whom Brad also loves so dearly," you might begin, again starting with an "I" statement. "I hope I can be part of this family closeness. We want so much to share our lives with you."

Summing Up

Dozens of conflicting emotions play themselves out in these very first weeks and months of your new relationship with your in-laws-to-be. You're excited, you're scared, you're nervous, you're thrilled. You're starting at a clean slate, with no idea of how it will be filled in the coming years. You do know that the most important business of this stage is to lay the foundation for a healthy, open, and sharing relationship, one of mutual respect and admiration if not love and warmth. You are starting to realize that certain themes—control versus independence, for example—will crop up again and again in endless variations as this relationship grows, expands, and matures. As we explore the very early stages of marriage in the next chapter, you'll see how couples struggle to establish themselves as adults, and what role in-laws can play in this process.

CHAPTER TWO

Growing Up—and Away

More than age or occupation, marriage moves you along in the life cycle from adolescent to adult. A young couple, newly engaged or married, is heavily invested in trying on this new role and showing it off like a new set of clothes. She signs her name on a check for the first time, he gets a bank loan in both their names. It feels good.

No matter how old you are, until you couple in a socially accepted way—that is, get married—your family may have trouble seeing you as an adult (and, if the truth be told, it's often hard to see *yourself* as an adult). During courtship and engagement, every member of your family has to begin to experience every other member in a new way, in a new role.

In these new roles, you will be dealing with a wide range of bewildering issues—issues of parental control versus independence; of loyalty to a parent versus bonding with an in-law; of romantic expectations versus stark reality. As you are taking these very tentative first steps into the next stage of your life, your new in-laws are also struggling. Their challenge is to walk that fine line between stranger and family member, often with no experience with this new balancing act. Meanwhile, your own parents are coming to grips with the fact that the child they nurtured and played with is entering into a covenant with another person—and may soon have a child of her own to nurture and play with.

Even if your parents may tentatively start to recognize you as an adult for the first time, they're still feeling a certain tension, a certain push-pull, surrounding some issues.

Debby, a small-boned brunette with a melodic voice, came to see me, full of conflict and uncertainty. An eighteen-year-old college student in Philadelphia, she was engaged to Charles, nineteen. Although Debby's parents lived out of town, Charles's folks lived nearby—*too* nearby, if you ask Debby.

"I guess I should feel lucky that Charlie's parents feel so close to us, but what I'm really feeling is smothered," she said plaintively. "Last winter we got season tickets to the Philadelphia Orchestra. When I told Charlie's mom, Joan, about it, she ran right out and bought tickets for the same performances, same nights, one row behind us!"

Debby was furious, to say the least. Feeling insecure about establishing herself in a new school and a new community, missing her own parents thousands of miles away, Debby felt that Joan was forcing herself on her, trying to cultivate a relationship that had barely had time to be planted, let alone to blossom. Joan brought food to her apartment, offered to do her laundry for her, insisted that Debby come shopping at Joan's favorite boutiques.

Ironically, Debby wasn't having trouble winning independence from her family of birth—it was the family into which she was marrying that was giving her grief. In her case, the struggle for individuation was playing itself out on her future mother-in-law's turf.

For her part, Joan was bewildered by what she saw as Debby's rejection. Charles was her oldest child and only son; she felt it only natural to become close to the woman he was marrying. She had embraced her daughter-in-law-to-be, she had welcomed her warmly and without reservation, and *this* was the thanks she got: Complaints from her son that his fiancée was feeling "crowded." And all her loving gestures were being met with coldness and defiance.

When Debby's own parents announced that they were coming East for a visit, the young woman was just thrilled. But by this time she so resented Joan's very presence that when she made plans to entertain her parents at dinner, she refused to invite her future mother-in-law. A friend of Joan's who heard about the dinner arrangements told her about them, and Joan and her husband showed up—uninvited.

Telling me about the incident the following day, Debby was outraged that Charles's parents had "crashed" her party. But as she gradually calmed down, she began to realize that she had been wrong. Very wrong. With my encouragement—and with equal measures of trepidation and embarrassment—Debby went to see Joan to apologize.

It was a big step, and it marked a turning point in their relationship. "I'm going to make a lot of mistakes," Debby told the older woman. "I'm eighteen and you're forty-three. So when I make mistakes, you tell me, and I'll try to listen. And when you make mistakes, I'll try to tell you."

Joan accepted Debby's apology with grace. She recognized the risk the younger woman had taken in speaking so frankly and with such vulnerability. The courage Debby showed helped Joan see her more as the adult Debby so fervently needed to be.

And what of Joan's need to be so much a part of her future daughter-in-law's life? Wasn't she confusing being loved with being needed? We all know people like Joan, who want so much to feel needed that they push themselves on others without realizing the effect they're having. While it looked as though Joan was being controlling and intrusive—it certainly *felt* that way to Debby—she was actually trying to befriend the younger woman in the only way she knew how.

Instead of letting the situation get more and more tense, Debby should have made her feelings known by creating an occasion when the two women could come together to talk. "I appreciate very much what you're doing for me," Debby might have said gently, "but sometimes I feel a little, well, smothered. I want to be with you, spend time with you, but sometimes I just need a little space."

While Debby's case was unusual because it was an *in-law* who was having trouble separating from a younger relative, the circumstances will probably be familiar to most of you who are parents. It *is* hard to let go of a child. Even the most well-intentioned parent sometimes needs to be reminded that her "little boy" or his "little girl" is growing up, and has earned the right to be treated like an adult.

Feelings of Disloyalty

Kathy and her future mother-in-law, Laura, had hit it off from the start. Even Kathy's fiancé, Joe, remarked about how well the two women got along. They shared the same taste in clothes, enjoyed the same music, and even liked the same brand of cranberry herbal tea. But soon Kathy was feeling a little . . . uneasy about the way the relationship was going.

"I like Laura a lot, she seems like such a nice person," said Kathy, a dental hygienist. "But I'm worried that my mother might be jealous. When Laura invites me to lunch, I always try to invite my mother along, or else I say no. I'm afraid if I like my mother-in-law too much, my mother will be jealous."

Whether the young woman's relationship with her own mother has been warm and loving or stormy and tumultuous, the issue of disloyalty often rears its head in these weeks and months before the wedding. As all parties struggle to define the new family configurations and the way each person fits in, there's bound to be confusion, worry, and misgivings.

If you've been close to your mother as a child and then as a young adult, it's very normal to worry that a growing relationship with another older woman might threaten your mother—and the warm bond you share with her. And if you've had a troubled relationship, you might see in your growing closeness with another woman a future wedge dividing you and the mother with whom you've always yearned to share intimacies and loving gestures.

In either case, now is the time to do a little reality checking. First, to get a clue about how your mother is really feeling about all this, take a look at her relationship with her own mother-in-law. Are the two older women close? If so, that can be a clue to you that she'll easily accept a loving relationship you enter into with your own future in-law. If, on the other hand, your mom and *her* mother-in-law fought like cats and dogs or just barely tolerated each other, this might be the time to talk about it with your mother: "How come you and Grandma Eloise never got along? Do you think I'll have the same trouble with Sam's mom?"

Next, get a handle on whether your own fear of losing your mother is making you worry about the disloyalty issue. Maybe you're "projecting" your feelings onto her, a common way of coping with problems. If this really is a case of what psychiatrists call "projection," if you're ascribing to her the feelings that are really yours, then the issue of disloyalty flies out the door: "If my mother is not worried about my being disloyal to her, then why should I be?"

Often, though, it's not that easy to reach this realization on your own. You may need to solicit another opinion—your father can provide a good ear at this point. Gently sound him out about your mother's feelings: "Dad, do you think Mom is upset that I'm spending so much time with Kirk's family, especially with his mother? I don't want her to be jealous."

Then, too, it helps to go right to the source—your mother. Talk to her directly, tell her what you re thinking, and reassure her that your relationship with the new woman in your life in no way encroaches on the special tie you share with her. Some hugs and kisses at this point wouldn't hurt, either.

What if you're the future mother-in-law? Be aware that this sort of conflict is common, and might be eating away at your son's fiancée. You may have to be especially understanding for a little while, as she works things out with her own mother. Proceed with caution here; pushing your future daughter-in-law for closeness and warmth at this point could be dangerous. She's walking a fine line here between you and her own parents; she needs some space to balance herself on that line with no undue pressure from outside. And she'll love you even more if you give her that space.

Make Room for Mother-in-Law

If she had not already married off two sons, Jayne would have been completely baffled and discouraged when she encountered Lauren. A self-composed and friendly woman of fifty-two, Jayne had a warm and open relationship with the wives of her two older sons. Jayne spoke several times a week with her daughters-in-law, and enjoyed getting together with them to visit art galleries and play golf. But when her "baby," Jeremy, took a bride, Jayne felt as though she'd struck out. Twenty-year-old Lauren wanted nothing to do with her new mother-in-law. All of Jayne's overtures—invitations to lunch, to the theater—were met with the same polite but distant reply: "Sorry, but I have plans with my mother."

And indeed, Lauren and her mother, Frances, *were* spending a hefty amount of time together. Shopping, the movies, late afternoon tea—every minute Lauren could spare from her job as a school librarian she devoted to Frances, even six months into her marriage.

"Nothing I do seems to work," a frustrated Jayne said to me, after yet another call to Lauren was rebuffed. "No matter what I try to do, I can't penetrate that twosome. It's as though they're glued at the hip!"

Nor did appeals by Jeremy to Lauren seem to help. When the young husband tactfully suggested to his bride that it would be nice if she would take the time to have lunch with Jayne, Lauren would bristle. "You're just trying to get me away from my mother," she would pout, and then would call Frances.

The wall of impenetrability Jayne was facing, and the frustration she was feeling, were the basis of a problem that is common in early marriage, especially if the new wife is fairly young, as Lauren was. The fact that she was a woman barely out of her teens, yet to develop much of a sense of "self," was the key to both her excessive dependence on her mother, and her almost total rejection of her mother-in-law. To put it simply, Lauren was afraid Jayne would "swallow her up." Although Jayne was warm, friendly, and outgoing, Lauren was intimidated by her—and the way she chose to deal with that intimidation was to close the older woman out of her life.

It's not uncommon for a mother-daughter relationship to be close. That wasn't the problem. What created the resentment here was the young wife's refusal to allow her mother-in-law to play even the smallest role in her life.

What can you do if you are a mother-in-law facing this type of situation? First of all, you have to be pretty patient. You need to give your daughter-in-law some time to mature and to realize that allowing another woman (you) into her social circle will neither destroy the relationship she has with her own mother nor cause her to lose her own identity.

While you're waiting (and it's tough, I know), don't give up making the effort to become her friend. Keep extending those invitations, and don't act hurt, insulted, or angry when she demurs. Rather, speak to your daughter-in-law warmly, praising her for her accomplishments and recognizing her strengths: "Jeremy told me that you got a promotion at work—I'm delighted for you and proud of you." With words like these, you let her know that you are not a harsh and critical mother-in-law (remember the stereotypes!), but rather a woman who wants to be close with her. Not a threat, but a source of comfort and support.

Let your daughter-in-law know, in little ways, that she is important to you. She may test this attitude—calling you at inconvenient times such as dinner or during a business meeting you're conducting—but it's essential that you give her the unspoken message, "You are valuable to me. I have placed you high on my priority list." Taking the time to talk with her at inconvenient times reinforces that message.

Try some alternate ways to engage your daughter-in-law, such as including her in an "all-girls" night with your other daughter-in-law, or inviting both her and her mother out for midmorning coffee if work schedules permit. Show her that you're willing to be flexible to encourage her to be part of your life.

NOTE: *Don't*, however, try to enlist the help of your other daughters-in-law in bringing in the reluctant one. This is a sure route to family disunity, and could very well backfire. She may bitterly resent their meddling, and see it as an extension of your trying to "intrude" into her life.

By the same token, it's risky to ask your son to intercede. Forcing him to side with either you or his wife is likely to create an intolerable tension in his marriage, and could even drive a wedge between you and him—or between him and his wife. Far better to tell him that you'll find your own way through this situation, and urge him *not* to become involved.

When Expectations and Reality Clash

After an exciting and romantic courtship, Jason, a reporter on a local daily newspaper, took Erica home to meet his mother, Harriet. The older woman, mother to four sons, welcomed Erica, an administrative assistant, with a warm bear hug and unabashed enthusiasm. "Finally," Harriet exclaimed, "the daughter I never had!" Erica, soft-spoken and well-mannered, was thrilled at the instant rapport—at first. She was delighted when Harriet laid out the plans she had for the two of them: They'd go shopping together at the mall, Harriet would help Erica pick out some new outfits, they'd have lunch. "This will be so much fun," Harriet told her. "Over tea we can tell each other *everything*."

Then Erica started to get a little nervous. A competent, independent young woman with a very close relationship with her own mother, she wasn't looking for the kind of relationship Harriet envisioned. As Jason's mother began bombarding her with more and more plans—"I've made reservations for lunch at my favorite restaurant. Wait till you try their clam chowder!"; "I know this wonderful dressmaker I want to take you to; she'll make you the perfect dress for your engagement party!"—Erica found herself shell-shocked and responded to the barrage by withdrawing completely. It was the only way she could maintain her own space in the face of Harriet's unrealistic expectations.

The notion that your future daughter-in-law is going to be the daughter you never had is a common one. Jason's mother had painted in her own mind a picture of the perfect mother-daughter relationship—with a woman who was not her daughter, would never be her daughter, and did not *want* to be her daughter. In the end Harriet was only setting herself up for disappointment—and setting Erica up for frustration and a feeling of being smothered. The situation also made Erica constantly fear that she was disappointing Harriet—not the ideal way to conduct a relationship.

Future brides or young wives can also fall into this trap of harboring unrealistic expectations, and not just regarding their in-laws. Many a woman has a kind of idealized picture of the man in her life—that he will protect her and shield her against harm and outside intrusion. This belief comes from social conditioning, from a lifetime of fairy-tales revolving around a dashing Prince Charming who charges in on a white steed and promises to "take you away from all this."

Later, when Prince Charming stands idly by as his mother "invades" your kitchen to make her son's favorite chocolate cake, reality kicks in and fantasy takes a tumble. He's not going to "save" you from the invading monster—that's his mother, and she's making his favorite cake! He's no dummy.

Often, when unrealistic expectations enter the in-law equation, it's not a matter of who's right and who's wrong; it's more a matter of how to deal with the ensuing disappointment when the expectations are not being met. Human nature being what it is, the most common tactic is to find someone to blame. It's frequently easier to blame the one furthest removed—the in-law. It's easier and safer, too, because you don't risk losing the son or daughter in whom you're so emotionally invested.

So, when your husband "fails" you by not standing up for you when your mother-in-law wants to commandeer your kitchen against your will, the natural tendency is to point your finger at your mother-in-law. When "the kids" haven't called you for three weeks running, you mutter, "It's my damned daughter-in-law's fault!" In both cases, your expectations haven't been met, so you're looking for someone to shoulder the blame.

It's a natural human tendency, but in the long run it's not particularly productive. What you really need to do is align your expectations with reality.

How can you do this? Try the following tactics:

1. Determine who is really disappointing you.

   It's not easy, but this means being almost brutally honest with yourself. If you've not got that call from your son and his fiancée a hundred miles away, it may *not* automatically be her fault. Don't jump to conclusions. Do be ready to confront your child.

2. Re-examine your expectations.

   If you thought that all mothers-in-law took their daughters-in-law to lunch once a week, and yours doesn't, pinpoint the source of that notion and ask yourself if it is viable. Did you watch a television drama that laid out that scenario? A television commercial? Did a friend tell you that *her* mother-in-law takes her out to lunch weekly? Then ask yourself honestly if this ideal is the only model of a good mother-in-law.

3. Look at the larger picture.

   Okay, so she *doesn't* take you out to lunch, or buy you gold hoop earrings, or get you orchestra tickets to the opera. But she's loving and considerate, and she makes a mean pot roast. Okay, so your future daughter-in-law won't agree to be a surrogate daughter. But she's a terrific listener, she's agreed to come visit with your son every Sunday, and you have a hunch she'll make a wonderful mother. In short, rather than focusing on what's *not* there, look at what *is*. All too often, if we come into a relationship with a narrow mind-set, with a fixed idea of what's to come—and it doesn't materialize—we're inflexible and bitter. If you can open yourself up to new possibilities, you're more likely to find something positive and worth savoring in the reality, rather than ruing the dream.

Living with Someone Else's Expectations

On the other hand, what if you're the victim of someone else's unrealistic expectations? That's what happened to Lois, a fine-boned brunette of fifty-four whose son Steve had just become engaged to a lovely woman, Andrea. Andrea came from a dysfunctional family. Her mother suffered through countless hospitalizations for back problems, and her father was abusive. The young woman told Steve that she couldn't wait to become a member of his family. She was looking for the mother she never had, to pick out her clothes, to teach her to cook, to share her most intimate thoughts.

Lois, who had already raised two sons and a daughter, wasn't looking for yet another child. She adored Andrea, she enjoyed spending time with her, and was thrilled that Andrea was going to be part of her life, but she was just as glad to pass on the nurturing role. Lois was looking less for a maternal relationship than for a peer relationship.

If you find yourself in Lois's awkward position, your job is to disengage yourself gently and understandingly. It's flattering to be thought of as the mother she never had, but unless you're willing to donate a great deal of time and emotional energy to the project, you're doomed to failure. You have your own life and your own interests, and the right to pursue them.

Instead of falling into the surrogate-parent trap, Lois had to follow the same procedure she had used when it came time to separate from her own children: Support their independence by giving gentle little pushes out of the nest. She had to make herself available to Andrea to give advice, but not to solve the younger woman's problems; to introduce Andrea to young women her own age and encourage her to develop independent friendships; to suggest that Andrea explore her own interests as a capable and functioning adult, while pointing out that she, Lois, was doing the same.

Just Say No

In general, when you're a victim of someone else's unrealistic expectations, it's important to recognize the situation early on. How do you know if the expectations are unrealistic? Simply because the other person is demanding more than you feel comfortable giving. If, after you've done a careful evaluation of your feelings and the situation, you do conclude that your future in-law is asking too much of you, recognize that it's okay to say no. Politely but firmly: "No, I can't make it every Sunday and Thursday for dinner." "No, I can't fix dinner for your boss and his wife."

Just say no. Saying yes or maybe is dangerous—it gets you deeper into the stew and sets you up as the heavy if you don't carry through. Far better to refuse tactfully and diplomatically early on than to promise something you don't intend to deliver.

Now, what if you are the daughter-in-law and your expectations of the ideal mother-in-law are not being met? This is also a common situation, as Adrienne, a plump redhead who managed an office, found out. Adrienne and Keith were married in a storybook wedding; they'd known each other for many years, and their parents had been close friends for over forty years. Adrienne went into the marriage expecting a warm and close relationship with Keith's mother, Blanche. The young woman had been very close with her own mother, and she saw no reason why she couldn't attain the same intimacy with Blanche.

From the beginning Adrienne was disappointed. She and Keith bought a house near his parents, but it seemed as though Blanche, busy with a full-time job at a nearby bookstore, never had time for Adrienne. Telephone calls went unreturned, invitations went unacknowledged, and Adrienne complained bitterly that any time she asked her mother-in-law out to lunch, the older woman had better things to do. Adrienne quickly formed a mental image of Blanche as self-centered and selfish. Never mind that Keith's mother always brought some nice trinket for Adrienne whenever she did visit; never mind that she expressed great interest in Adrienne's work and in her participation in a little-theater group. Adrienne was looking for more. She was looking for Blanche to treat her not like a daughter-in-law, but like a daughter—to be completely wrapped up in her life and to drop everything when Adrienne called.

Adrienne's expectations were clearly out of line, and I told her so. Blanche did not raise her, she did not have the same ties to her that Adrienne's own mother had. If you suspect yourself of sharing Adrienne's behavior, take a moment to analyze the situation. Initially, it might not seem as though you are being unrealistic, but stop to look at your in-law's relationship with her own children, and her history of relationships in general. If she is warm and loving to others and not to you, then you probably are justified in expecting more. If she treats you with the same affection and respect that she gives to others, but it's not enough for you, then you must look inward. Often, knowing that no personal insult or intent to slight was meant makes you feel better about the situation. You may regret that you don't have the relationship you dreamed of with your mother-in-law, but you won't blame her or yourself. And often with that insight comes an easing of the tensions that accompany unmet expectations.

What Do I Call Them?

Helen had spent a pleasant evening baby-sitting for her two grandchildren. When her son Allan and his wife, Sarah, returned from the movies, she gathered her things together and left, not noticing her blue sweater still draped over the back of the sofa. When Sarah saw it minutes later, she dashed out of the house to catch up with her mother-in-law and return it.

Reaching the street, Sarah saw the older woman a short distance away. She was walking leisurely toward the bus stop. Sarah hurried after her. Hearing someone behind her, Helen recognized her daughter-in-law's footsteps, but did not turn around or acknowledge her in any way. Instead, she started walking faster.

Sarah doubled her speed, trying to reach her. Helen walked even faster. Soon the daughter-in-law was racing to catch her husband's mother, who seemed oblivious to her presence.

Puffing and panting, Sarah finally called out, "Helen!" to capture the older woman's attention. Her mother-in-law stopped abruptly. At last she turned, then smiled at her out-of-breath daughter-in-law. "I'm glad you finally found something to call me," she said with a grin. "Helen is fine with me."

In these early days of a relationship, the question of what to call the in-laws looms as a major issue—maybe *the* major issue as a relationship gets off the ground. Names are the way we relate to society as a whole and to individuals on a one-to-one basis. When we deal with someone who doesn't address us by our correct name, or who calls us by a name we don't like, we feel that we don't matter, that we are being discounted, or even worse, insulted.

That's what was happening with Helen and Sarah. Like so many fiancées, brides, and newlyweds, Sarah had put off confronting the question of what to call her mother-in-law until the whole issue assumed a life of its own.

Few decisions facing newly engaged couples are as thorny or as delicate as the question of what to call the spouse's parent. It is this issue that can set the tone for the entire relationship to come. Sarah's situation was typical; although she and Allan had been married seven years, the problem went back to the very early days of their engagement.

From the start, Sarah didn't feel comfortable calling Helen "Mother" or "Mom." She felt that doing so would be disloyal to her own mother, whom she loved very much. It also felt oddly intimate to refer to a woman she didn't know well by these terms. Not sure what to call this woman in her life, Sarah resorted to a very common solution: She didn't call her anything.

Helen reacted to Sarah's dilemma in a very typical way—she felt growing resentment about not having a name. She felt spoken *at*, not spoken *to*. For her part, Sarah felt awkward and uncomfortable about appearing disrespectful to her elder. The longer the situation dragged on, the more embarrassing it was for all involved, and the more reluctant everyone was to bring the issue out into the open. Until the incident at the bus stop *forced* it into the open.

A woman who never establishes a name for her mother-in-law all too often winds up talking to her through other people—or, more tragically, not at all. She unwittingly sets up a sort of "triangulation," whereby she talks to her mother-in-law through a third party—often the son/husband. "Joe, tell your mother we can't make it this Christmas." "Joe, tell your mom we'll be there at eight for dinner." Not only is this awkward, as you can readily see, but it also shortly ceases to be a problem just between mother-in-law and daughter-in-law. The entire family can be dragged into the unspoken conflict.

It starts out innocently and benignly enough, as Joe begins to speak for you more and more, until the whole thing assumes the aspect of a charade. There's an awkward tension; no one wants to acknowledge that you have not come to grips with what to call Joe's mother, and everyone else in the family tiptoes around the void. Joe's sisters and brothers and their spouses may begin to talk about it behind your back, and they may start to feel annoyed or even manipulated by the situation. Soon, what started out as a simple choice over what to call your mother-in-law has escalated into a family brouhaha.

Talking about names is a good place for you and your future in-law to begin building a relationship. In many cases, it offers the first serious look at how open both parties are to forging new ties. Why, then, is this such a source of tension?

Fear of rejection is a key element. You might be afraid that if you urge your son's fiancée to call you "Mother," the younger woman will resent the forced and artificial closeness such a name implies. Or she might worry that using your first name will sound disrespectful. So you keep silent, and the situation is allowed to drag on. You hold your tongue for fear of provoking a confrontation, and your daughter-in-law struggles along, resorting to an uncomfortable "Um, er . . . ah" when forced to speak with you face to face.

If this all sounds depressingly familiar, don't despair—there's a solution. Instead of fumbling along, or trying to dodge the issue, negotiate directly. The younger person might ask, "What would you like to be called?" The future mother-in-law then could express her preference: "I'd like to be called Mom." Or, "I'd be comfortable if you called me Lena."

Rebecca, a client, said that her wedding shower, her fiancé's mother approached her and said, "Now is the time to start calling me Mother." It was awkward at first, Rebecca recalled, but the fact that the older woman had broken the ice made it easier to make the name adjustment in the days and weeks that followed.

I've found that most new mothers-in-law want to be that forthcoming, but it's not always easy and involves taking a certain amount of risk. It might help if you're in this situation to offer your daughter or son's future spouse a choice: Please call me either Mother, or Mom, or Lillian. That way, if the younger woman calls her own mother "Mom," she can opt for the name that doesn't present a conflict of loyalties. Sarah, for example, might have felt more comfortable calling her mother-in-law "Mother Helen," or some variant that didn't sound exactly like the term she used for her own mother.

Your fiancé or new husband can play a large role in making things easier for both you and his mother. He may be the one to approach her and explain the discomfort you are feeling, to share with her your feelings of awkwardness that the word "Mother" invokes. You may also be shy; you might be worried about showing disrespect either to your own mother or to this new woman in your life; there very well may be something in your upbringing that prohibits this new intimacy. Having your new mate make that clear to his mother can go a long way toward soothing hurt feelings, especially if he handles it diplomatically and with sensitivity.

Your fiancé can also be the one who sets the tone when he makes the initial introductions. If he has talked about this issue beforehand with his parents, he might let you know that they prefer a more informal approach from the outset by introducing you like this: "Grace, these are my parents, John and Mary." This puts everyone on a comfortable footing right from the start.

Although your son is the first line of defense, if for some reason he doesn't do his job properly, it becomes your responsibility to give his fiancée some choices. You have it in your power to set the tone for this new relationship. And it's to your benefit to speak out early and to be as flexible as possible. If you have your heart set on being called "Mama," and that's the term your future daughter-in-law has used for her own mother for twenty-six years, you'd best be prepared to accept "Mom" or some nickname she likes—or be doomed to a life with no name.

If you're grappling with the name issue, try not to get too worked up. Most couples *do* come to an understanding that's comfortable for everybody. Plenty of people use first names for their mothers-in-law and fathers-in-law; many adjust to calling them "Mom" and "Pop." Whatever you do, relax, use your manners, make your feelings clear, and resolve the problem early on. If the transition still hasn't taken place by the time of the wedding, take comfort in this: The arrival of children will probably make the entire issue obsolete. I've yet to meet a mother-in-law who objects to being called "Grandma."

More Name Games

I've found that the issue of names can crop up in quite a different way when, for one reason or another, a woman opts to retain her birth name. This decision often prompts feelings of bewilderment on the part of a mother-in-law, who wonders (sometimes with resentment) why, if the family name was good enough for *her*, her son's new wife chooses not to accept it.

In the case of Tia Webster, a young telephone sales representative, her decision not to take the name of her new husband, Mal Adams, seemed to sit well with Mal's mother, Libby, until five years after the wedding, when Tia shared this painful incident with me:

"I was lying in my hospital bed, just hours after giving birth to a beautiful baby boy, whom we had named John Adams-Webster. Libby came into the room with gorgeous roses, kissed me on the cheek, and left immediately to see the baby. Not five minutes later she was back in the room, shrieking and carrying on. When I finally got her to calm down, she looked at me in a rage and said, 'How could you do this to me? How could you give this baby—*my* grandson—*your* name?' "

Tia was still livid months after the bitter words were exchanged, and she told me that her mother-in-law's little scene had ruined what should have been one of the happiest days of Tia's life. Her experience reinforced for me the need to address issues such as these very early on in a relationship, so that they not be allowed to go underground, only to crop up painfully when you least expect them to.

This is an issue best handled together by future wife and husband. In Tia's case, she and Mal had never sat Libby down and told her of the younger woman's decision to keep her birth name, and pass it on to her child. Worse, whenever Libby mentioned the subject to Mal, he shrugged it off with a nonchalant, "Don't worry about it, Ma." Nor had the couple taken pains to correct Libby gently when she repeatedly sent them anniversary cards addressed to "Mr. and Mrs. Mal Adams." Instead, Tia just put the cards away in a red velvet box without comment to her mother-in-law about her choice of names.

The situation would not have got so out of hand if Tia had urged Mal to take a firmer stand, letting Libby know how important it was to his wife to be called by the name she had chosen, and how comfortable he felt with her decision. And at holiday and anniversary time, Tia could have diplomatically reminded her mother-in-law that although Libby had chosen to accept *her* husband's name, Tia had taken a different path—and that neither woman's choice was better than the other.

When older women complain to me that their daughters-in-law have "rejected" their son's names, I remind them that the younger women have an identity that is very important for them. Often they have established themselves in careers in which their original names carry some weight. Whatever the reasons behind the choice, it is certainly not a rejection of the name . . . or of the mother-in-law.

When the Wedding Turns into a Hassle

Stephanie Mason was in tears. Her parents wanted to give her a small garden wedding on a Sunday afternoon, inviting maybe fifty people, tops. They planned to invite twenty-five family members and friends, leaving twenty-five slots open for Stephanie's fiancé, Christopher Burke, and his family. The Masons were quiet people, not wealthy but comfortable.

The Burkes, on the other hand, were socially prominent and well-connected. Mr. Burke was on the boards of many influential financial institutions, and Mrs. Burke volunteered on the auxiliaries of half a dozen area hospitals. Their idea of the proper wedding for their son was a black-tie affair on a Saturday evening, with a large orchestra playing at an elegant downtown hotel. Guest list: three hundred people.

Christopher's parents were more than willing to pay for the extra people, because it was important for them to have a more elaborate affair. As his mother said plaintively, "After all, when will I have another chance to dance at my son's wedding?"

Guess who was caught in the middle? Christopher was happy with the plans Stephanie's parents were making, but felt some allegiance to his parents. Stephanie understood her parents' financial limitations and their pride in giving their daughter the best wedding they felt they could afford. On the other hand, she also desperately wanted to please her future in-laws . . . not to mention her future husband.

Large wedding or small intimate affair? Black tie or blue jeans? Catered sit-down dinner or hot dogs and baked beans from a buffet table? For an event that lasts maybe five hours, a wedding comes complete with an inordinate number of decisions, all of them fraught with meaning. Who makes these decisions often constitutes the first face-to-face struggle between in-laws. Not only *who* makes the decisions but *how* the decision-making process is played out, and how flexible the players are, can set the tone for years to come.

A wedding is a public declaration, not only of the bride's love for her bridegroom and vice versa, but also of the social status of the parents, their place in the community, and their sense of style. How they marry off their son or daughter becomes an outward display of the family's worth and accomplishments. And woe to the bride or groom who stands in their way.

Conflicts can arise over almost any decision: whose name goes on the invitation, what colors the bridesmaids will wear, where and what time of day the ceremony will be held. Often, differences of opinion arise over who will pay for what at a wedding. Traditionally, it's been the responsibility of the bride's parents to bear all the costs (except those of the honeymoon, usually a gift from the groom's parents), no matter how prohibitive. Even the language of weddings—"giving the bride away"—places the obligation squarely on *her* family's shoulders. And if they're footing the bill, the conventional wisdom goes, shouldn't they have the final say over where the affair is held, who gets invited, what is served, and who sits with whom?

Alas, as Stephanie Mason found out, it's not that simple. The groom's family has an equally emotional investment in the nuptials. And, they may argue, if they are willing to contribute the bucks—and many, many families of the groom are willing to go dutch these days—shouldn't *they* have an equal voice?

That's how the Burkes felt. They believed they weren't asking for anything unreasonable—just the chance to entertain three hundred of their friends, family, and business acquaintances. At their own cost. They were willing to compromise on the day and location of the wedding—the Sunday afternoon garden party was acceptable; not terrific, but okay—but they would not budge on the numbers.

The conflict over a wedding can be this outright, or it can be more subtle; so subtle, in fact, that the parties involved don't always realize there is a power struggle being waged just below the surface. The source of conflict may be where to hold the wedding, when to hold it, even what colors the attendants should wear. In Stephanie's case, the numbers were only the more visible issue here. The hidden agenda was: Who is going to make the decisions in this family—Stephanie and Christopher or Christopher's parents?

The Burkes began applying gentle pressure by offering to pay for the additional guests they wanted at the wedding. They felt their offer was generous and considerate and that it would solve the problem completely. Stephanie's parents felt her prospective in-laws were butting in where they didn't belong, taking the wedding out of their hands and trying to wrest control of the whole affair. Stephanie and Christopher just watched in despair, becoming more and more torn over which set of parents to please. What should have been an exciting and thrilling time for the young couple became sour and filled with tension.

Finally, Stephanie couldn't hold out any longer. She convinced her parents to accept the Burkes' contribution and to invite the extra guests. But she gave in reluctantly, with a lot of hard feelings. Feelings that were likely to persist into the early years of her marriage—and perhaps beyond.

Heading Squabbles off at the Pass

What might families do from the beginning to avoid the dissension and the disagreement that can so color an upcoming marriage? An early face-to-face meeting involving all parties in the wedding would have been the most logical first step; it would have allowed both sets of parents to lay their cards on the table, but even more, it would have allowed both the Masons and the Burkes to feel that they had a forum for their respective points of view.

Such a meeting would also have made the engaged couple feel less like go-betweens in a process that was getting increasingly away from them. It would also have given Stephanie and Christopher the chance to come together as a couple, to support each other, and to present a united front. This would have helped them establish their own identities as a family—a crucial step for any engaged or newlywed couple.

Negotiating strategy doesn't differ all that much from boardroom to living room. To kick off the process, each side presents its point of view, with background and information about what has gone into the decision-making. Stephanie's parents, for example, could have talked about how important it was to pay for their daughter's wedding themselves. They would have had the opportunity to be honest about both their financial limitations and their emotional investment in the wedding.

For their part, the Burkes could have talked about how important it was for them to accommodate their social obligations, and why they felt moved to extend themselves to pay for the greater number of guests. And Stephanie and Christopher? Now would have been the time for them to reaffirm their love for *both* sets of parents and for each other, and to emphasize that their wishes and needs when it came to the wedding were of equal—if not greater—importance than those of their parents.

In the Mason/Burke encounter, one solution might have been to have a wedding in keeping with the bride's family's circumstances, followed by a post-honeymoon reception hosted by the groom's family. Then *all* parties could have felt satisfied, all could feel that they came out of the bargaining session with their needs met and their dignity intact.

Summing Up

The beginning is a difficult time in any relationship. You are feeling one another out, trying to be on your best behavior and to make the best-possible impression. It's a time that combines the joy of discovering qualities you like about the other person and the disappointment of realizing she or he is not perfect.

In these few tentative weeks and months, it's imperative to recognize potential problems quickly and to take steps to minimize them. All of you have an equal stake in making this in-law relationship work; all of you have an equal responsibility in making sure that it does.

Now is a perfect time to do some self-exploration, to analyze how you appear to others and what you expect from the relationship you and your new family are building. It's a time to be brutally honest with yourself and to realign your expectations if they have no ties with reality.

It's also a time for honesty and openness. You have to be willing to share with your new in-law what you need and what you want from this new bond. I firmly believe that if you tell people how to please you, they'll be willing and even eager to do so. Or at the very least, they'll try.

The best way to make your feelings known is to start with an "I" sentence: "I would really like it if you . . ." For example, you might say to your future daughter-in-law, "I really like it when *you* call me on the phone, and I always want you to feel comfortable calling me." Or you might say to your future mother-in-law, "I would feel more comfortable if you would call before you drop over. It lets me plan ahead a little." Using this type of "I" sentence is nonaccusatory and nonthreatening, and gives the hearer more a sense of cooperating than of bowing to a demand.

It also helps at this crucial time to be aware that everyone comes to a relationship with some pre-set notions and ideas. The beginning few months are a time to make those expectations mesh with reality. As you spend more and more time with your new in-laws, and learn more about them as individuals, the fantasy will start to fade, and the reality will take over. You will see your in-laws less as a repository of dreams—a cardboard character of what a mother-in-law or a daughter-in-law is *supposed* to be like—and more as multi-dimensional people.

This process will play itself out countless times in the course of your relationship, as roles and family situations change. You may have a fixed set of ideas of what a grandparent is, for example, a set of ideas that will be forced to change as your mother-in-law becomes a flesh-and-blood grandmother and not just your *concept* of what a grandmother is. Again, you will have to analyze the issues and adjust your reality. Meanwhile, your mother-in-law will be doing the same as *you* become a parent yourself, and she will have to deal with her own fantasies and notions of the ideal mother.

What's important at every juncture of the relationship is to see each other as individuals, as real-life people with real-life qualities. And to realize that just because this is your fiancé's mother, or just because this is your child's fiancé, you don't have to love this new person in your life right away. You may come to adore your child's spouse, or you may never warm up. But try not to prejudge. A little tolerance buys a lot of goodwill between new in-laws.

CHAPTER THREE

We're Only Just Beginning

Arthur, the dark-haired manager of a men's clothing store, and Elizabeth, a petite redhead who works as a computer programmer for a large bank, have been married less than a year. Before the wedding, they had had Sunday brunch at Arthur's house every week. The whole family came—Arthur's brother and sister and their spouses and children. The extended family would sit for hours over coffee and Danish, rehashing old times and formulating new plans.

The fact that the brunch was a weekly command performance wasn't something Elizabeth loved, but she was reluctant to make waves before the wedding. When she did mention to Arthur that she might like to free up the day for something else, Arthur always reassured her that things would get better after the wedding. Since she was eager for her future in-laws to like her and accept her, she went along with the status quo.

Almost a year later things hadn't got better. Elizabeth was

beginning to feel antsy, to say the least. She wanted Sunday mornings for couple time. She and Arthur both worked at demanding jobs, and they used Saturday to catch up on errands and to exercise at their respective gyms. Sunday was the only day of the week they could sleep late and make love leisurely, without looking at the clock.

But with family tradition so firmly established, Elizabeth felt uncomfortable about speaking up. She complained to Arthur, who was reluctant to tamper with a ritual that had been part of his life since childhood. Elizabeth was very persistent, so one Sunday morning Arthur and Elizabeth came late for the brunch, arriving when dessert was being placed on the table. Another Sunday morning they called at the very last minute to say they wouldn't be there. One way or another, they failed to play their part in the family tradition. The tactic they opted for—passive resistance—forced the issue further and further under the table. Not only did the problem continue to exist, but their way of tackling it created guilt on their part and resentment on the part of Arthur's family.

Welcome to the wonderful world of the newlywed, where the name of the game is establishing yourself as a couple while navigating the dangerous waters of conflicting demands, contrasting expectations, and competing needs. And that's just between husband and wife. When in-laws enter the game, the stakes go up—and the pay becomes all the more risky.

In the opening days, weeks, and months of a marriage, wife and husband are engaged in a delicate ballet à deux, learning to read each other's needs and to accommodate each other's desires. This is a time when you're likely to be establishing yourself in a career or already making your mark in your chosen field, while also grappling with such thorny issues as whether to buy or rent a house, whether to go back to school for a graduate degree or to stay on the career track, or whether to have children now, later, or not at all.

All of these struggles are played out against the backdrop of developing in-law relations. You, too, as a mother-in-law, are struggling with your role in all this: Should I offer advice or should I keep still? Would the benefit of my own experience be helpful to my son or daughter-in-law, or are the newlyweds best off finding their own way—even if they stumble? You are also feeling your way on such issues as how often to invite the newlyweds over, how often it's all right to call them, or, if they're young, how much financial assistance (if any) to offer the struggling kids.

Picking and feeling your way through the land mines of early marriage, both as the new bride and groom and as the new mother-in-law and father-in-law, is the challenge you're facing now. Like the period that preceded it—the days leading up to the wedding—this new stage has its pleasures . . . and its pitfalls.

Among the issues we'll be tackling in this chapter and the next are how to decide who makes the decisions in a family—and how once you've reached them, to reinforce those decisions. How much input will you allow your in-laws to have in major matters; how much *should* they have? We'll talk about time, and how it's allocated: Marla's parents want the newlyweds to spend their first Christmas with them; Roger's parents want the couple to spend the holiday with *them*. Where is King Solomon when we need him?

Where You've Been, Where You're Going

The wedding is behind you now, and along with the photos in the white satin-bound album and the faded and dried yellow roses from the bridal bouquet, you've got the beginnings of a new stage in your in-law relationship. If you've all got off on a solid footing—fabulous. If not, don't panic. At this point, nothing is written in stone. The relationship is still relatively new, and still relatively pliable.

It's a good idea to take stock about now, to get a handle on where you stand with your in-laws and where you're headed. A quick quiz will give you an idea of how things are progressing—or not progressing, as the case may be. It's set up for either newlyweds or in-laws, so just check off the appropriate answer.

1. Do you feel anxious when (your children, your in-laws) visit? YES _____ NO _____
2. Are you angry when your (son, husband) talks about his (wife, mother)? YES _____ NO _____
3. Do you get a headache when you spend time with (your children, your in-laws)? YES _____ NO _____
4. Are you always late for an engagement or family event when (your children, your in-laws) are involved? YES _____ NO _____
5. Do you feel uncomfortable because there's been no resolution of the name issue? (She still calls you "Um, er . . ." You still can't bring yourself to call her "Mom" or anything else.) YES _____ NO _____
6. Do you and your husband fight when (your children, your in-laws) are around? YES _____ NO _____
7. Do you fight in private with your husband over (your children, your in-laws)? YES _____ NO _____
8. Do you dread time alone with (your children, your in-laws)? YES _____ NO _____
9. Do you find yourself complaining to your friends about (your children, your in-laws)? YES _____ NO _____
10. Do (your children, your in-laws) ignore you? YES _____ NO _____

SCORING: If you had 10 "no" answers, your mother-in-law or daughter-in-law is Mother Teresa and you've got my heartiest congratulations. Eight "no" answers? Your relationship is on solid footing. The lines of communication are open—keep doing what your doing. Four to six "no" responses? Fair to middling. Go back over the quiz and pinpoint where the weaknesses are; knowing where you need help is the first step toward making things work better. Zero to four "no" answers? You have serious trouble, and this is the time to begin putting some real effort into making this relationship work.

If you've answered half or fewer of the questions with a "no," start redoubling your efforts at building a strong and trusting relationship with your in-laws. Do a reality check: Am I falling down on the job? Are my own expectations out of line? Bring in your spouse at this point to help you determine whether your feelings are justified: Does *he* feel intruded upon by his parents? Does *he* feel the children are ignoring you? Does *he* feel he's spending a lot of time and effort defending his parents to you? Does *he* feel there's a reciprocal relationship here—that they come to you as much as you are expected to go to them?

If he doesn't agree with you that you have a problem, then you may need to reevaluate your own feelings; to go back over what you perceive as a problem and determine whether it is, indeed, a problem, or if you are being too judgmental or expecting too much.

Understand, also, that even if your husband doesn't agree with you that the relationship is in trouble, it doesn't mean you *don't* have a problem. He may have his own reasons for not acknowledging that difficulties exist. Denying a problem allows him the luxury of doing nothing about it, of not getting involved, or not having to confront his own feelings—or in the case of the younger generation, of not having to confront his parents.

Many men may not even realize a problem exists in the way

you and his parents relate; *he* may have related to them in this way for ages, and it seems fully normal and healthy to him. The things that bother you—his father's incessant telephone calls, his mother's suggestions that your job is not as important as your husband's—may not annoy or dismay him as much as they do you. (Understand, also, that it's not your job to change your husband's relationship with his parents. He's had decades of relating to his mother and father in a certain way—your role is not to interfere with that in any way.)

What if he *does* agree with you that your relationship with your in-laws leaves something to be desired, or you yourself feel that it does? Then it's time to give and get some feedback right from the source. Using a series of "I" statements, approach your in-laws directly and openly and express your needs, desires, and concerns. Start with the general—"I would like our relationship to work; is there something I can do to make it better?"—and move to the specific—"I like it when we have dinner at our house sometimes instead of always at yours. What are your thoughts about that?" "I feel sad and as if you don't like to talk to me, because whenever you call, you ask right away to talk to Henry. Could we spend a few minutes together on the phone?"

This approach will put the problem squarely on the table, and will allow each party to look at it from his or her own perspective. It's very possible that your mother-in-law might not have realized what she was doing when she called repeatedly and asked for her son without giving you the time of day. Phrasing the complaint in the form of an "I" statement lets her know—gently and nonthreateningly—what she's doing and how it affects you. Then it's up to her to take the initiative to make things right.

What if she doesn't? That's a very real possibility. Sometimes she's just not going to hear you—literally or figuratively. Do you give up trying? Complain to your husband? Neither tactic will change the situation. Rather, just keep going back to her with your "I" statements, hoping that at some point your request will take. I'm sure you'll feel better at just having expressed yourself.

SETTING LIMITS

As the two of you are forming your new nuclear family, you are also setting its boundaries and borders. You are determining what gets through those borders—and what stays outside. Setting limits protects a couple from intrusion from the outside world, and helps husband and wife bond together as a unit.

In dealing with such issues as your time, your finances, and your personal life, the more well-defined the boundaries, the healthier the relationship. In these early weeks and months of married life, you're deciding how much *time* to spend with others, and how much to reserve as couple time. You're deciding whether to try to make it alone financially, as a couple, or to accept a little help (*money*) from one or both sets of parents. You're also debating the issue of *information*: how much to keep to yourself and how much to share.

The ability to set limits is an important prerequisite to feeling good about yourself. Allthough this is an issue for all people, it's frequently harder to set these limits when you're not clear about the closeness of the relationship at hand. When you're at the beginning of a relationship that you hope will last a long time, you may be reluctant to take a risk by saying no. You are still trying to be polite and find the proper balance among the roles of family, friend, and stranger.

The familiarity you feel with your own family is just not there yet with your new relatives. When it's your own sister, for example, who has made a demand on you, it's easier to refuse because you've learned from experience that saying no sometimes is okay, and that in your history together it's been balanced by yes. In this burgeoning relationship with a new in-law, however, you're still searching for just the right balance.

Younger couples who have not had as much experience setting boundaries may need more practice than those who have been on their own for a while.

How to start? It's not easy for most of us, especially women, who have been taught to please others and to put our own needs second or third. If you find yourself having trouble saying no—to an in-law's repeated requests that you spend time with him, to a barrage of questions you consider too personal to answer—try these techniques:

1. Practice with a friend.

   Role-play situations that give you an opportunity to say no. For example, a good friend plays your father-in-law, who asks you to lend him a book you're still in the middle of reading. Or your friend pretends to be your sister-in-law, who asks you how much you paid for your new dining-room set. Play the situation out as many times as you need to feel comfortable with setting the limits that make *you* comfortable.

   If you are like most people, you already engage in such "role play" regularly, perhaps without knowing you are doing so. You rehearse in your head what you'll say to your boss when you ask for a raise, or you compose dialogue aloud when preparing a business presentation. These role-playing techniques I've suggested are just extensions of those everyday exercises.

2. Reverse roles.

   Replay the same situations, this time with *you* playing the in-law role. Watch how your friend sets limits, and see if you can pick up new techniques and tactics.

3. Imagine the worst that can happen if you say no.

   Ask yourself: What am I afraid of if I say no? Is it that you think your in-laws couldn't handle it—or that *you* couldn't? If your in-laws can't handle the rejection, focus on the type of relationship you have and ways to make that "rejection" less painful. You might try saying no, but pairing it with something positive. "Mom, we can't come for dinner every Saturday, but we *can* come once a month. Would you like me to bring a fruit salad when we come on the fourteenth?" Adding the "no" to the fact that you'd like to be more accommodating gives your in-law something pleasant and positive to grab hold of in the midst of your demurral.

4. Try saying no in easier situations.

   If the thought of saying no to one of your in-laws terrifies you, work your way up to it gradually. Try refusing when a friend asks you to lunch, or seeks you out to do a favor you feel would put a burden on you. Practice on your own sister or mother. With every experience of saying "no" to others it should become easier to say "no" to an in-law. *Then* start little by little saying no to your mother-in-law's less important requests—for example, if she asks if she can borrow your green-and-gold scarf. Once you're on comfortable ground, you can work up to refusing politely when she asks you and your husband to spend a week with her at the seashore.

   In the beginning, saying no—after a lifetime of saying yes—feels awkward and uncomfortable. But if you do it, you'll find out something amazing: People don't stop loving you because you sometimes say no. Many times, in fact, your honesty will win you more respect. And as you get more of what *you* want out of your relationship, you won't feel taken advantage of or overpowered. This in turn will gain you more self-confidence and more respect from your in-law—and enhance your limit-setting abilities. Remember: You have the right to say no *and* yes, not just one or the other.

How do we know what our boundaries should be? A lot of our knowledge comes from our families of origin, and the way they did things. Our families are our models; watching the limits our parents set in their relationships with others teaches us how to set limits with others. If, as a child, you were taught to respect the fact that Mommy and Daddy needed private time together, you'll know it's okay for you as a newlywed couple to have the same type of private time.

Boundaries also arise from your own comfort level. You know what makes you feel right and what makes you feel intruded on, invaded, crowded, exposed, vulnerable, resentful, and angry. These emotions are signs that let you know—compellingly—that it's time to throw up a barrier. All of us have an inner voice that tells us what's good for us, what's right. And we have to learn to trust that voice.

As children, we sometimes learn to mistrust these hunches when we're told that our feelings aren't valid. But the more we come to trust that inner voice, the louder it gets. And if you are feeling that your in-laws are expecting too much—*trust that voice. Act on it.*

As a couple, you have to learn to set these boundaries early and firmly. Inappropriate limit-setting or the inability to set boundaries is a common problem in dysfunctional families; it leads to breakdowns in communications and inappropriate behavior. For example, the young married who recounts to her mother how many fights she and her husband had last week or describes in detail his sexual inadequacies is revealing details that are too intimate to be shared between the generations. Such a situation leaves the young wife vulnerable, and the mother feeling uncomfortable. Just as parents shouldn't discuss their fights and sexual lives with their children, so adult children shouldn't bring these issues into the living rooms of their parents.

The same is true for the mother-in-law: She shouldn't ask about intimate matters in the marriage.

Setting Informational Boundaries

Parents often feel that they have a right to ask anything and get an answer. After all, you're their child, and they have spent decades taking care of you. While you were growing up, it was natural for your parents to ask all types of questions—Did you finish your homework? Did you brush your teeth this morning? Did you take your vitamins?—and to expect a response. Old habits are hard to break, even if you—the child—are now married and living with a wife or husband. But now the questions are a little different: "How long is Kevin going to work for Jones, Smith and Mathers before they make him a partner?" "Where are you going on your next vacation?" And the killer: "When are you and Roberta going to make me a grandmother?"

Sylvia, an outgoing receptionist at a large law firm, was delighted when Matthew, a car-phone installer, came home with the announcement that he'd gotten a raise. That evening, talking with her mother, Claire, on the telephone, she shared the news. Claire was delighted for her daughter's good fortune. "So, how much is he making now?" she asked. Taken aback by the question, Sylvia didn't really know how to respond. She was uncomfortable sharing what she felt was personal information, but she didn't want to hurt Claire's feelings. "Well," she finally hedged, "we're just really pleased."

What might you do if you find yourself in this type of situation? This could be a good time for you to start setting some limits. "Mother," you might begin, "there are things that Matthew and I would rather keep between us, and I feel uncomfortable sharing his salary with you."

As part of a couple, your challenge is to be clear about when you're willing to share information and when you're not. You, as the parent, should pay attention to clues that your child is establishing some boundaries, and you should try to respect that. This also requires trust on your part—trust that you have done a good enough parenting job so that your child can make sound and mature decisions. If you don't have this trust, you might create the type of problem Marsha and Tony faced.

Married for two years, Marsha and Tony saved scrupulously, even fanatically, for their own home. Both felt strongly that they wanted to pick the home out themselves—it was a personal decision and their first major purchase as a couple.

Marsha's parents, the O'Malleys, had bought and sold several houses in their thirty years of marriage, and felt they had much expertise and experience to offer. They were full of pointers: "Don't buy a split-level; you won't get your money's worth." "Look into adjustable-rate mortgages; they're your best bet if you're just starting out." The more advice they offered, the less Marsha and Tony wanted to hear. They resented what they saw as an intrusion on the part of her parents, and they came to see it as the O'Malleys' effort to take the decision away from them.

Eventually, the struggle for power intensified to the point that whenever the older couple asked how the home search was going, Tony and Marsha would clam up. Gatherings became strained as both couples avoided the topic, and relations deteriorated quickly. Finally, in desperation, Marsha and Tony bought a house just to have the ordeal behind them. But it was a rundown handyman special in a decaying part of town—and they overpaid, to boot.

Now each couple is blaming the other for the disaster. Tony and Marsha say bitterly that if the O'Malleys hadn't interfered so much, they wouldn't have felt so pressured to make a decision. The parents, throwing up their hands in dismay, say this is proof that "the kids" aren't financially responsible and don't know anything about real estate and home buying.

Both positions are justified. Tony and Marsha felt understandably trapped and boxed in by her parents' repeated advice. They were both adults, and both had good jobs, but the O'Malleys' intrusiveness had made them feel childlike and inadequate. They wanted input, but not inundation. Yet they didn't know how to say to the older couple, "This far, but no more."

What might they have done? Early on, they could have established a pattern of asking specific questions: "Do you know anything about Society Hill as a place to live?" "What are the advantages of a colonial over a ranch-style home?" This would have given the O'Malleys insight into the process of decision-making that the younger couple was using, showing that they are capable of making decisions on their own, and capable of doing research, but that they still valued and sought the O'Malleys' wisdom. It also would have placed boundaries around how much of that wisdom they were willing to accept, limiting the older couples' participation in a way that kept Tony and Marsha comfortable, but still giving the parents a feeling of being needed and valued.

And the O'Malleys? It would have been helpful if they had picked up the clues the younger generation was sending their way—the changes in behavior, the reticence to share information, the chillier atmosphere when all four were together. Given the clues, they could have recognized that they were in forbidden territory. Tony and Marsha were well into adulthood, and had earned the right to make decisions on their own.

What if those decisions are less than wonderful? So be it. That's how couples learn. It would be helpful if parents could look back on their own shaky beginnings and remember—with a touch of wry humor, if possible—some of the mistakes they made when they were just starting out: He spent their savings on a beat-up old convertible that he just *had* to have; she pawned the coin collection to buy a new stereo. A mistake can be something to laugh over for years—and it can also be something to learn from for years.

It also helps you as a parent to remind yourself of the decisions your child has made in the past that have turned out well—choosing good friends, spending his allowance wisely, selecting the right courses in high school. Remembering how fortunately these smaller decisions worked out helps you let go more easily when bigger ones arise.

In the final analysis, it comes down to trust again: letting go enough to give your child and his/her spouse the freedom to fly. It's hard, I know. If you let them make the little mistakes, though, they'll have the confidence and the courage and the decision-making skills to avoid the big ones.

Money Makes the World Go Around

In one of my classes entitled "Human Life Cycles," I ask the students to finish the following paragraph: "Susan came in first in her medical-school class." Tell me about Susan, I say—what did she do after that? How did she live her life?

In their written responses, almost all of the students head in the same direction: They define Susan's success in terms of dollars and cents. "She became a famous orthopedic surgeon and bought a large Victorian mansion and had it decorated with antiques," one young woman wrote in a recent class. "She bought a Rolls-Royce and took a month's vacation in the South of France," a male student wrote. Cars, boats, luxury hotels—this, for them, is the definition of success.

In our society, money equals power, control, status . . . success. Not only is money one way we measure how well we're doing in the world, it's also the most common and pervasive way, the standard against which all else is judged.

Because of the power we invest in it, money can become a tool for manipulation, a source of conflict between spouses—or between in-laws. The scenarios are endless: Florence and Richard, buying their first home, might ask to borrow money from Florence's parents, who are living on a fixed income and feel reluctant to part with their "nest egg." The Morrisons might give a large financial gift to their son Harvey and his wife Dina, but completely ignore their daughter Lisa and her husband Nick. The Jordans might feel strongly that they want to pay their daughter Amanda's law-school tuition, while Amanda and her husband, Frank, feel equally strongly that they don't want to accept the money.

Just as couples have to learn to set limits on information-sharing early on in their wedded life, so, too, do they have to come to grips with the issue of money. They must also reach the understanding that those green-and-white pieces of paper represent much more than just buying power. They represent raw power, too.

Bonnie was a bright and friendly woman from a comfortable suburban background. She was used to getting elaborate gifts from her family—some might even have called her pampered.

Her husband Jonathan, on the other hand, had always struggled for every penny. He had worked his way through school and started his own computer-repair business. His philosophy was that you have to work hard to earn the good things in life. He felt distinctly uncomfortable with Bonnie's family's way of life—and of spending.

The difference in beliefs was never as dramatically played out as during an incident over a car, about three months after their wedding. The couple clearly needed a second car for Bonnie to get to her job as a buyer in a small boutique. They had been looking at small economy cars until Leon Thompson, Bonnie's father, stepped in. Armed with a supply of rational arguments—"A larger car is a better buy. It'll last longer, and you'll get a better deal when it's time to resell"—Bonnie's dad offered to purchase the young couple a luxury car that was light years beyond their budget. Bonnie was thrilled; Jonathan was dismayed.

Not only was the young husband annoyed at what he saw as his father-in-law's intrusion in his life, but he was also bitterly hurt at the implied suggestion that he couldn't provide for his wife. Bonnie, on the other hand, looked at things in a more practical way: if her father had the money and wanted to buy her a nicer car, why not? They were her parents, and they had always bought her nice things. That didn't undermine Jonathan's ability to provide for his family, Bonnie said.

"It's impossible for me to get through to her about this," Jonathan said. "But I'm afraid that if we say yes to the car, Bonnie's folks will keep on wanting to give us more and more, and I feel pretty strongly about our standing on our own two feet."

How do you solve a problem like this? You begin by defining the problem and deciding whose issue is at that problem's core.

Whose Issue Is It, Anyway?

When setting limits in any category—money, time, information—it's important to determine if the issue regards (1) you personally, (2) facing you as a couple, or (3) your combined in-laws. Sometimes, of course, the issue can cross over into all categories, but more often it belongs to just one. Knowing whose problem it is can help you reach a solution.

Is it an individual's issue? Had Bonnie been listening to Jonathan with her head and her heart, instead of just her ears, she would have heard him talk about his pride in "making it" as a couple on their own; she would have heard his fear of not living up to his own expectations of being a good provider for his wife. Then she could have separated what dad's offer meant to her from what it meant to her husband, and she could have based her part of the decision on a fuller understanding of the whole picture.

Is it a couple's issue? Perhaps the car represented only a small piece of the whole—perhaps Bonnie was relying too heavily in general on her parents to support her and her husband, even if only emotionally, in the first few weeks and months of married life. Now would be the time for Jonathan and Bonnie to sit down and talk over some of their feelings about the situation, being honest and using "I" statements as much as possible: "I feel worried that your dependence on your parents is creating distance between us." "I am hurt that I have the chance to have a fancy new car, but you see it as interference by my parents."

Talking it over, allowing both spouses to vent their feelings as well as their points of view, helps a couple put the problem into perspective and deal with it thoughtfully and calmly.

Is it an intergenerational issue? All too often, gifts like the automobile Mr. Thompson wanted to give Bonnie come with strings attached. "There's no reason why you two can't come and visit more often, now that you have such a nice new car" is one possible message, either spoken or unspoken. Or, from the parent who offers to pay for graduate school for a married son or daughter, another message might be: "Sure, I'll pay for your graduate degree. But you have to choose the school I want you to go to, in the field I want you to study." The underlying theme in these instances is that the one who provides the money wields the power.

The use of a gift—be it money, items, or services such as childcare—as a tool for manipulation erodes trust among in-laws. If a gift comes with strings, you have three choices. You can refuse it flat out. You can accept the gift with all its stipulations and play by the giver's rules. *Or* you can negotiate. You can say, in essence, "We will accept the (car, tuition money, sofa, whatever), but not the strings that come with it."

In short, you can set limits: "Thank you for the car, Dad, we both really appreciate it and it will make our lives so much easier. But we'll only take it if you realize that it doesn't mean we can come over more often. We'd love to see you more, but our jobs are so demanding right now."

As well, the recipient has to come to grips with the fact that accepting a gift does not diminish one's independence, nor does it turn feelings of affection and caring into feelings of need. This is a common fear among new couples—Jonathan expressed it succinctly when he said, "I'm afraid that if we take the car, we'll become more and more dependent on Bonnie's parents." It's not so. A gift, when given in the right spirit, can be simply an expression of love and warmth, nothing more.

A Promise Is to Keep

Michele's father-in-law, Curtis, was a well-connected businessman with a hearty hail-fellow-well-met air about him. Shortly after Michele and Pete got married, and she began looking for a job in the advertising field, Curtis approached her and promised that he would talk to his contacts at the city's top ad agencies and help her line up a position. The young bride, newly out of college, was excited and elated. At Curtis's suggestion, she held off looking elsewhere and waited for her father-in-law's contact to come through.

It proved a long wait. A month went by, and nothing happened. Michele shyly asked Curtis how things were progressing; Curtis repeated his promise that he would set something up "as soon as possible." Meanwhile, the young couple was having difficulty making ends meet on just Pete's salary as a law clerk for a judge, and Michele was getting more and more nervous.

Another month went by, and still nothing happened. Michele would devour the morning newspaper and its columns of want ads, but reassured by Pete that his father "would come through," she did nothing to follow up on any of the leads.

More time passed, and every time Michele asked Curtis what was happening, he repeated the same refrain: "These things take time." Finally, when she pinned her father-in-law down in a desperate face-to-face encounter, Curtis admitted that he felt uncomfortable "hitting up" his colleagues at the present time. "It's not a good time, there have been certain business reverses. . . ." And so on.

Michele was furious. When she calmed down, she put out some feelers of her own, and eventually landed a job at a midsize advertising firm known for its creativity and imagination. It doesn't take much imagination to figure out what the entire episode did for the budding relationship between Michele and her father-in-law. A little thing called trust seemed gone forever.

Here are some ways to avoid the same fate:

1. Don't offer anything you don't want to or can't deliver. The only thing your in-law can judge you on is your word. Promising to be a dependable baby-sitter for your daughter-in-law when she wants to go back to work and then not being available is not a way to develop a trusting relationship.
2. If asked for assistance, think it over. It is better to tell your in-law that her request to borrow your car for a month is something you really need to consider than to say a quick okay and live to regret it. Give a definite time frame: "How about if I let you know in a week?" Then examine the pros and cons of the request—and how granting it will affect you. If you honestly think the request is too burdensome, allow yourself to say no.
3. If you say yes, or if you make a promise, don't tie the gift or the help to any strings. Offering to underwrite your son's and daughter-in-law's August vacation only on the condition that

they spend it with you is a cheap trick. You may get that month with them, but you won't have won any favor in their eyes.

LIVING ON BORROWED...CASH

Polonius might have given Hamlet some priceless advice in Shakespeare's classic when he urged him, "Neither a borrower nor a lender be." However, there may be times in any in-law relationship when it becomes necessary to be one or the other. When it does, there is a right way and a wrong way to go about it.

Maureen and Derek have several thousand dollars saved toward a down payment on a house. They're putting the money away prudently from their weekly paychecks; he's a physician's assistant for an ambulance company, she is an executive secretary at an insurance company. Suddenly, the perfect house has come on the market: a three-bedroom colonial with covered patio and large backyard. There's only one problem: They have only half of what they need for the down payment. So they look to Maureen's parents, the Sullivans, for a loan.

At this point, a little preparation and a little planning can be indispensable. From the very start, this "loan application" has to be handled with tact, dignity, and respect. Here's how:

1. Make the request the same way you would approach any lending institution.

   As you would if you were seeking money from a bank or a savings and loan, you must offer full financial disclosure. The prospective lenders (in this case, your in-laws) have the right to the information they need to "process" the loan, and the children have the obligation to furnish that information. As much as your in-laws may love you, it's *their* money, and they have the right to protect it.

2. State the terms of the loan and how it is going to be repaid.

   "Mom and Dad, we need about five thousand dollars by March 31, which we hope to repay over four years in monthly payments of one hundred dollars. The payments will be in cash or check, whichever you prefer." Making the terms as clear and as up-front as possible averts entanglements down the road, and also informs all parties in the transaction of exactly what to expect.

3. Anticipate any difficulties and try to plan for contingencies.

   Nobody wants to lose his job or break his leg or watch as a tornado rips off the roof of his house, but these things—and worse—do happen. Now, at the very beginning of the loan process, is the time to talk about potential tragedies and how you'll deal with them. "If Franklin loses his job and we still owe you seven-hundred-fifty dollars, may we come to you for a moratorium on loan payments?" is a wise question *before* Franklin loses his job. Again, knowing what is expected smoothes the way later on.

4. Approach your in-laws with respect throughout the transaction.

   You wouldn't walk up to the loan manager at First City Federal and demand money. You wouldn't whine, wheedle, cajole, or beg. You wouldn't accuse—"You've *never* been there when I needed you," or "You always loved my brother better than you loved me." Just because these are your parents or your in-laws with whom you're dealing, the same rules apply—maybe even more so. Because while a bank loan can be repaid in five, seven, or ten years, and chances are you'll never see the bank officer again, it's a different story with family. You'll be sitting down to dinner with them often over the next decade; keep that in mind when you approach them for that loan.

Rules for the Lender, Too

What if you've been hit up for a loan by "the kids"? Certain unwritten rules govern your behavior here. Of course, the choice is yours as to whether you will come up with the money or not. If you do, provide that money with respect. Remember, it's a loan, not a license. As long as the terms of the agreement you've reached are met, you have no right to complain or interfere in the younger couple's life. Lending Roberta and Jack money for a down payment doesn't mean you can tell them where to buy, what to buy, or how to buy. It doesn't mean you can force your decorating ideas on them or criticize their choice of sofa or drapes. It certainly doesn't mean that you can pry into their personal lives and demand to scrutinize their checkbook. Once that loan is made, and the payments are coming as promised, all obligations have been fulfilled.

Moving In

Elyse and Lance had lived in three different cities while they completed their schooling. Now, with their degrees under their belts, they were ready to settle down, and they agreed that the best career opportunities for both of them existed in the Boston area, where Lance had grown up and where his family still lived. His mother, Trudy, realizing the financial crush the young couple was in, invited them to stay at her house until they found a house they could afford. Everyone involved thought it would be a matter of weeks. The weeks stretched on to months.

Statistics tell us that increasingly the empty nest is not staying empty. Adult children are flocking back to live with parents at a rapidly growing rate. In many cases, they are also bringing their spouses.

Almost always, the reasons are financial. There has been a job loss, or they have decided to go back to school for an advanced degree. Sometimes the move is planned, sometimes it is not, but the net result is the same: A couple winds up living with one set of parents, and a whole family of problems moves into the nest with them.

Quite often, the older couple has been adjusting happily to the pleasures of being on their own after two or more decades of parenthood. They've got used to coming and going as they please, to eating when they want, to relaxing around the house in just a robe . . . or in their underwear. Although they are generous enough to open their home to their child and spouse, they know they will be making sacrifices of time, of privacy, and of freedom.

The transition can be tough, for them and for the younger couple, who now are guests in someone else's home. Although everyone knows that the situation is temporary and that the young husband and wife are saving money to buy that house down the road, it's still a strain.

What can you do to ease the inevitable tensions? First and foremost, set rules ahead of time. All parties should have a crystal-clear sense of what is expected of them: What rooms are off-limits? Who does the cooking and who does the laundry? When should the television be turned off at night, and when is it too late to make a telephone call? Who pays for the groceries and who gets to drive the one car that's not in service?

Whether the stay is for one week or one year, the key word here is "compromise." Each family member should be prepared to give a little and get a little so that no one suffers a lot.

You're used to eating dinner—preferably Italian—at six, when you and your husband get home from work. Your in-laws prefer to dine at eight, strictly low cholesterol. You would just as soon fend for yourselves at the earlier hour; your in-laws insist on everyone coming together later for dinner as a family. What do you do? Compromise. During a discussion, you all decide that on weekdays, when everyone is working and patterns are easy to establish and adhere to, you'll eat together at seven, with a menu of fish, chicken, and veal—no butter. On Friday, Saturday, and Sunday nights, it's each couple to themselves; you'll go for your beloved pasta in oil and garlic early in the evening, and they'll stick to their nonfat foods at a more fashionable hour.

When entering into this type of discussion, it's essential to remember the Golden Rule of Houseguests: It's the hosts' house. They may be your in-laws, but they are also your hosts, and all the common rules of etiquette apply:

- Respect their privacy as scrupulously as you would want yours respected.
- Ask to borrow a book/comb/bottle of aspirin/clock radio before just assuming you have a right to an item or a piece of clothing because it's in the house.
- Let your in-laws know your schedule and your comings and goings, so they can plan meals and leisure time accordingly.
- Respect their property; don't put your sneaker-clad feet on your mother-in-law's spotless white couch.

For the hosts, too, there are certain responsibilities. It's up to you to let your daughter and her husband know what's expected of them. Don't succumb to the feeling that you have to "entertain" them constantly—this can only put a burden on both couples. Give them a chance to have some desperately needed time alone. Treat them like the adults they are. It's easy to fall into old patterns that were established so many years ago, but resist at all costs the urge to criticize your son's clothes or ask him if he brushed his teeth this morning.

Don't laugh—it's all too easy to get lured into this trap. That pertains to the younger generation, too. Often, an adult moving back into the family home falls prey to the temptation to revert to the comfortable role of son or daughter. Much to her irritation, Elyse found this happening when she and Lance were living with his parents. When they were on their own, Lance pulled his weight, sharing equally in meal preparation, cleanup, laundry, and general home maintenance. Now, after six months back in his mother's house, he was content to sit at the dinner table and be waited on. Instead of helping to serve the meal, he asked repeatedly for things: "Where's the salt?" "I need some mayonnaise."

"It's driving me crazy," Elyse said. "After dinner, he gets up and goes into the television room with his father. When I complain, my mother-in-law says, 'Leave him alone, he's tired, he worked hard all day.' What does she think I did all day—sit on my rear and eat chocolates?"

The longer the situation went on, the angrier Elyse got at Trudy, her mother-in-law. In addition to being furious that Lance was leaving Elyse with most of the housework, the young wife was terrified as she saw her strong, mature, and dependable husband turning into a demanding and whiny little boy right before her eyes. In her anger and despair, she directed her ire at the safest target: her mother-in-law.

Her emotion was misdirected—and worse, nonproductive. It was Lance who should have been on the receiving end of that fury, not Trudy. When Elyse did confront him, and explained her fears and her frustrations (as she had every right to do), her husband recognized what had been happening and began holding up his part of the marriage.

To avoid traps like these, you have to go into a shared living arrangement with your eyes open. For every advantage it affords—you save money on room and board, for example—it also has its drawbacks. *Both* sets of husband and wife are giving up something, whether it's privacy, independence, or a sense of freedom.

For all that you may be sacrificing, you may also be gaining something invaluable: the bond that comes from sharing your life closely with someone else. With a little planning ahead, a little courtesy, and a little common sense, you can use this period to make your relationship with your in-laws a warm and close tie.

Time, O Precious Time

One of the major challenges newlyweds face is allocating their time so as to satisfy everyone involved in the equation: themselves, his parents, her parents. It's a challenge they face while grappling with the issue of how they're going to carve some free time out of a hectic weekly schedule that often involves two full-time jobs, the upkeep of a house, night school or college classes—and the very real pressures of getting to know each other as individuals and as members of a brand-new family.

This is a reality for *any* couple, no matter how wonderful the relationship with his parents and parents-in-law. There are only so many hours in any given day, and so many in a weekend. If your basic belief is that everyone has to get an equal slice of your time—and, by association, of your love—you're setting yourself up for failure. You're never going to feel that you're meeting everyone's expectations. Sooner or later, you're going to have to learn that sometimes life's just not equal. Or fair.

In part, the faulty assumption that you can divide yourself equally often stems from the past, when customs dictated that a couple get married, go off on a two-week honeymoon to "bond," and then come back and join an extended family.

In the 1990s, adult children rarely live in the same state, let alone the same town, as their parents do; women have entered the work force in unprecedented numbers, and time is at a premium for everyone—including the mother-in-law, who's likely to have a full-time job or interests of her own.

Before marriage, it's likely that each spouse spent regularly allotted time with his/her family of origin. After the wedding, it's a completely different story.

The complaint I hear most frequently, from mother and mother-in-law alike, is, "Now that they're married, the children have no time for me. Before, we were busy with the wedding plans, we were shopping and getting ready, and now . . . now they've dropped me like a hot potato! To get them to come for Sunday dinner is like pulling teeth."

There's a good reason for this. In the first year of marriage a couple wants to spend most of their free time—what little there is of it—together and alone. Slowing down the social pace and spending time alone with just your new spouse is often a welcome change after the rigors of courtship and wedding planning. Since wife and husband are likely to be working hard at establishing or maintaining careers, putting in long hours and great amounts of energy, their "off" time becomes very precious to them. They may even begin to pull back from some of their closest friends in their effort to be together more. Bonding, I gently remind mothers and mothers-in-law, takes more than two weeks.

Couples often talk wistfully about wanting to spend more time with their respective families, but they resent any encroachment on their time alone. *She* says, "When I go to my parents' house, my mother wants me to sit in the kitchen and talk to her." *He* says, "When I visit my folks, my kid brother wants to pull me outside to play catch." *They* say, "We love both families very much, but why are they always trying to pull us apart?"

They're not. (Well, not in most healthy situations, anyway.) What parents are more frequently guilty of is seeing each partner in the new marriage as a child—*their* child—while the new husband and wife desperately want to see themselves as a unit. They want to be together, to make decisions together, to consider and be considered a cohesive *one*.

Thank Goodness Christmas Comes Only Once a Year

These wrenching demands on their time are a problem I see most frequently at holiday seasons, when both sets of parents are (wittingly or unwittingly) vying for their children's love and attention.

A cheerful and friendly brunette with intense blue eyes, Jill was anything but happy when she came to see me shortly after her first Christmas as a bride. Both her parents and Ryan's lived within forty-five minutes of the newlyweds. Without telling her, Ryan, the oldest of three children and the only one married, had gone ahead and made plans to spend Christmas Eve with his family. Jill's mother always made a large, traditional Christmas Eve dinner, to which Jill's two married sisters always brought their kids. That was the night all the nieces and nephews entertained the family with carols, and everyone exchanged gifts.

So Jill and Ryan fought. And fought. Both sets of parents—not unreasonably—felt the couple should be with *them* for the festivities, and the young couple agonized over their impossible choice. They wound up spending their first married Christmas at home, alone, barely speaking to each other. That left no one happy, not Ryan's parents, not Jill's parents, and certainly not Jill and Ryan.

It's not unrealistic for each set of parents to expect "the kids" to spend Christmas, Easter, Passover, or some other holiday with them. Can you imagine any parents saying, "No, we don't want you for the holidays this year?" Be assured that your folks *will* extend the invitation—and that they will be disappointed (but not fatally) if you turn them down.

Thus it becomes your responsibility, as a partner in a new and still-developing relationship, to decide how you're going to spend the holiday. Do it by sitting down with your spouse and considering the alternatives: "If we have Christmas dinner with your family, we can spend Christmas Day with mine." "We can have Thanksgiving dinner at your folks, and Christmas at mine." "This year we can go to your family for Christmas, next year we'll go to mine." "Maybe we can have them over to *our* house!"

The key here is for both of you to work on the solution together. Don't rush into any decision; be aware that logistics are often very difficult to work out—you're dealing not only with your needs and time frames, but also with those of your family and your spouse's family. Often this process will be as complicated as planning the invasion of Normandy—but not nearly as lethal once it's carried out.

A NOTE TO PARENTS: Be aware of the pressures and tensions your child and his/her spouse are feeling as Christmas draws near, and try to be understanding and supportive. The less you push, the more appreciative they are likely to be, and the easier it will be for them to reach a decision. Whatever that decision is, try to understand what went into it, and try to minimize the fear they may have about hurting you or the other set of in-laws. With luck, there will be other Christmases, other gatherings.

In fact, I urge in-laws and parents, in general, to respect a couple's need for time alone and their need to create their own traditions and holiday celebrations—not just now, but through the course of their marriage. There's no better gift you can give them than your understanding that they may want space and time to build traditions and rituals for themselves and for the next generation—your grandchildren.

One final word on the issue of time. I always urge newlyweds to respect each other's needs regarding relationships with his or her family. On the other hand, just because he wants to spend more time with his folks, doesn't mean *you* have to, also. Not all the time a couple spends with the older generation has to be as a couple. There's no reason why he can't satisfy his sense of obligation or his genuine desire to be with his father, for example, without you there. Just as you might like to have an occasional lunch alone with your father, shouldn't he be able to do the same with his mother? Sometimes arrangements like these take the pressure off a couple for "command appearances," and offer a wonderful chance to renew and refresh bonds that may have got strained over the past few years.

The novelist and cartoonist Mell Lazarus, creator of the comic strips *Momma* and *Miss Peach*, tells a wry and touching story of the very real conflicts a father-in-law faces in dealing with the young men who have assumed number-one status in their daughter's life. In the "About Men" column of *The New York Times* (April 5, 1987), Lazarus first describes the questions that plague him as he watches the newlyweds at the wedding of his first-born daughter: "Is he directing enough attention to her, or hogging it himself? Will the fact that he's 10 inches taller than she and has an inordinately loud voice allow him to dominate her? If it turns out that he will be earning the major part of their living, will that give him two votes to her one? And if he turns out to be a louse, will she know just how much she's obliged to endure? Does she know the first rule of marriage, the one that says it doesn't necessarily have to last forever?"

Okay, he promises himself, he will wait and see. Wait and watch.

Fast-forward ten years. At a gathering for Lazarus's fifty-eighth birthday, he is amazed to see one of his sons-in-law hand five dollars and the car keys to his wife—Lazarus's daughter—and say, without amenities, "We're running out of burger buns. Go get some while I shoot the breeze with my folks."

"She was pregnant with their second baby and for weeks had had what I saw as a tight line of fatigue across her eyes. She had also spent most of that day helping to prepare for the party. But I was astonished to see her cheerfully take the money and keys and start for the door."

Furious, Lazarus insisted on going himself for the buns. "By the time I got back from the market, I had worked myself into a full-blown rage. I strode through the house and out to the rear patio, threw the bag of buns at my bewildered son-in-law, and berated him loudly: "You idiot! How dare you order my daughter—seven months pregnant—around like a damned flunky."

As friends and relatives calmed him down, Lazarus slowly became aware of his breach. "In the awkward silence, the ugliness of what I had done came clear to me. My son-in-law was wounded and white-faced, two dozen relatives and friends were embarrassed, and worst of all, the daughter to whose rescue I had risen was in tears."

In the end, after the two men had hugged and Lazarus had made amends, all parties learned something about setting limits.

"To head off future explosions, I asked my daughters to try to understand my attitudes," Lazarus writes. "I told them that when they were infants, I vowed that only God would be in a position to help the man who treated them badly; he would answer to their father! And you're still my girls, I'm still your father, and your husbands are not exempt from that vow."

"Look, Dad," came the response from one of his three daughters, "if you ever see me with a black eye, call out the Marines. But until then, please don't worry." The same daughter took pains to tell Lazarus that he had completely misunderstood the party incident, that her husband's request had not offended her and that she would have welcomed the twenty-minute trip to the store as a break from the party.

"On balance," Lazarus sums up, "it's good that it all came to this. I feel better about my daughters' situations. They told me that their commitments are deep, and, when the need arises, they take pretty good care of themselves. And, at the same time, I got my orders: Don't march; stand down; Daddy, butt out."

Will he follow that advice? Lazarus ends his column with a cryptic, "We'll see." But knowing where the lines are drawn in a marriage, and having the good sense and the sensitivity *not* to cross those lines, goes a long way toward ensuring that the ties linking the generations do not become strangling bonds.

CHAPTER FOUR

AND BABY MAKES... COMPLICATIONS

The news that they are expecting a baby is a thrilling and exciting event in most couples' lives. It is a crucial milestone, marking the end of one chapter and the beginning of the next one. Bearing and nurturing a child teaches the family how to expand (literally *and* figuratively!) and how to integrate people into the family unit without losing a sense of themselves both as individuals and as a couple.

The same way that adding a child to the equation changes the relationship between husband and wife, it has a dramatic effect on relations between in-laws. Daughters-in-law and sons-in-law become mothers and fathers, mothers-in-law become grandmothers, and fathers-in-law become grandpas. Roles change, expectations change, needs change—and about the only thing you can say with certainty is that while baby makes three, baby also makes complications.

During the weeks and months while you're deciding whether or not to start a family; during the time when you're officially "trying;" during the early months of your pregnancy while you're experimenting with names in your head and your heart, you're going through a sea of changes—and so is your relationship with your in-laws. You're grappling with how much information to share with them and how much of their advice to accept; they're wondering how far they can nudge you when the urge to become a grandparent becomes overwhelming, and how much of their own childrearing experiences it's safe to pass on to you before you feel intruded upon.

That's what this chapter is all about. We'll explore together the problems that can arise—such as infertility and miscarriage—and the ways in-laws can help each other cope. We'll offer some solid advice on how to defuse potential hotspots, such as how to choose the baby's name (What do you do when your father-in-law says, aghast, "*What?* You're not going to name him after *me?*" And you'd sooner die than name that innocent baby Throckmorton Aloysius Ferdinand Smith III) and how to settle arguments over what/when/how to feed the baby.

For grandparents, we'll tackle what to do if your child and child-in-law suffer financial reversals and are forced to move back with you—lock, stock, and baby. How do you handle three generations under one roof without going *through* the roof? And what do you do when you've got a demanding, full-time job of your own, and your daughter-in-law begs you to baby-sit for little Tommy so she can go back to work herself? We'll talk about that old, rarely terminal but always painful ailment "grandparentitis"—the longing to become a grandmother or grandfather when you've got a child who isn't quite ready to deliver the goods.

The Grandparent Express

There's no question that the birth of a baby can forge new bonds between the generations and create a delightful third generation to love and cherish. However, more and more young couples in our culture are opting to postpone parenthood, for one reason or another. Although those reasons may be valid, appropriate, well-considered, and totally personal, the couples run the risk of being run over by the "grandparent express." They may learn to hate the familiar refrain, "So when are you going to make me a grandfather?"

For most couples, the pressure to produce grandchildren—whether it is subtle or strident—begins around the first anniversary. Before then, parents tend to respect your privacy as a couple regarding your childbearing plans. Once you reach that one-year mark, the lobbying begins in earnest. Sometimes it's covert: "Did I tell you that my best friend Jenny's daughter just had twins? They're adorable!" Sometimes it's not: "Doctors say it's best to have your first child when you're in your twenties. You'll be thirty in two years. . . ."

As the barrage intensifies, you and your husband can begin to feel under attack. You may feel that the power of decision-making has been stolen from you, and that the older generation is trying to call the shots. It's an uncomfortable feeling at best, particularly if you have no immediate plans to have children, and you are facing an organized lobbying attempt by would-be grandparents.

Statistically, women today are waiting longer to give birth to their first child. Twenty years ago, the norm was to marry and have children in your twenties. Today, it's much more common for a woman to wait until she has established herself in a career before she becomes pregnant—even if it means you're well into your thirties or even your early forties before you hold your first baby in your arms.

While your mother and mother-in-law may accept this—and even support it—on an intellectual level, that longing for a grandchild is a powerful urge. Even as you may be hearing the ticking of the biological clock, the older generation hears it louder and with more urgency.

The push to become a grandmother or grandfather can be as hard to resist as a tidal wave. Not only does the birth of that child move the entire extended family to another plateau of development, but it also brings with it the expectation of additional respect and reverence. A grandchild represents the continuity of life, and of family. It represents immortality.

Sometimes, the pressure to produce a child starts even before a young woman is married. This happened to Denise, an engaging, lithe blonde with high cheekbones. Although she was single, not involved with any particular man and quite content with her status quo, her parents, the Walterses, were pushing and pushing to become grandparents. "Sometimes I feel that they wouldn't even care who—or *what*—I marry as long as I produced a child," Denise said bitterly.

Then love struck, in the form of Alex, a sculptor with a flair for gardening. Denise and Alex were married after a short courtship. If Denise thought she'd felt pressure *before* the wedding, afterward she realized she had been dealing with novices. Now, the grandparent express was rolling in full force.

Ironically, Denise wasn't even sure she wanted children. She had a career as a museum guide that she loved, and she was studying for her master's degree in history at night. That, however, did not stop her parents from turning on the heat, pressing home their point every chance they had. Meanwhile, Alex was also coming in for his share of pressure from the Walterses, who were dropping not-so-subtle hints that maybe it was *his* fault that no baby was on the horizon. ("No one *else* in our family has had any problems," was his mother-in-law's repeated refrain.)

Denise felt confused, Alex felt besieged, the Walterses felt bereft, and no one was happy. After a year and a half of marriage, husband and wife were at each other's throats, and still her parents were whining, "So, when will we hear the good news?"

Clearly, something had to be done to break this pattern. I told Denise when she came to me for a consultation that the most important thing in dealing with her mother and father was to be honest about her feelings. Often, as in this case, parents don't realize the damage they can cause in their headlong rush to become grandparents.

The older generation has a very real stake in what the younger generation does, it's true, but parents need to realize that in many instances the best thing they can do is keep their own counsel. In Denise and Alex's situation, the Walterses' needs were interfering with the younger couple's life—with their day-to-day interactions, even with their sexual relations.

If you're caught in this type of trap, you have to approach your parents or your in-laws head-on, with gentleness and tact, reminding them that having a child is no one's business but your own, and that hinting, teasing, pressuring, and cajoling do more harm than good. It also helps if you can keep the parental haranguing in perspective, and not let it tie you in knots or cloud your own perspective. When to conceive a baby—or if—is *your* decision, no one else's. It's too important a choice to allow yourself to be swayed by someone else's needs. Finally, you and your spouse need to support each other with love and understanding while the external pressures are mounting. You must reassure one another that you've made your decisions about when to have a baby based on your combined needs—and that, in the end, those are the only needs that really matter.

If you're the mother or mother-in-law who's aching to hold your grandson in her arms, you have to keep one thing in mind: Your son or daughter and their spouse will produce a baby when *they're* ready, not when you are. That's how it should be. Think back to how you would have resented it bitterly if your parents had tried to dictate your own childbearing calendar. Act accordingly.

The Pain of Infertility

Robin is a thirty-two-year-old lawyer with deep-set gray eyes. Her husband, Benjamin, is thirty-four and also a lawyer. They have been married for four years—and trying unsuccessfully to have a child for the past two of them. They had met their first year in law school, seven years ago, and agreed when they got married that they would put off having a baby until both were well-established in their careers. Now, Robin is a successful deputy district attorney with several well-publicized wins under her belt, and Benjamin has a thriving law practice with two partners and an associate. They have a lovely ranch-style home with a large backyard, a large family room—and an empty nursery.

There's a special kind of despair reserved for the couple who desperately want to cradle a baby in their arms, only to fail in their attempts month after month. There are an increasing number of such couples today; an estimated one out of every five couples is facing infertility problems.

The period during which a couple is grappling with infertility can test the relationship among in-laws, as all family members grope toward understanding and mutual support. Communications often break down at this point, with would-be grandparents being the last to know that an infertility problem exists. Frequently, the couple has been so accustomed to dodging unwelcome questions about their pregnancy plans that the reticence carries over even when they've been trying to conceive for months or even years. For example, Robin and Benjamin had dodged the questions for years by saying to their parents, "When we decide to have a baby, we'll let you know."

Often, a couple's anguish over the failure to produce a grandchild—as well as the embarrassment over intrusive medical probing and poking they are enduring to determine the cause of the failure—also keeps them from sharing their thoughts at this sensitive time.

When they *do* break the unwelcome news to their parents, the couple—or frequently just the wife—can be bombarded with a barrage of unwelcome personal questions: How long have you been trying? When was your last menstrual period? How long ago did you last make love? What position did you use?

Robin, for example, found that when she told Benjamin's mother she was seeing an infertility specialist, the older woman demanded to know his credentials, his treatment plan, and why Robin wasn't seeing Dr. Sherman over at City Hospital.

Suddenly, the boundaries Robin and Benjamin struggled so hard to build and maintain as a married couple had come tumbling down, and they were facing a well-meaning but nonetheless painful invasion of privacy in addition to all their other grief.

For their part, the parents of the infertile couple may take the situation personally, blaming themselves for not producing a child who is perfect enough to reproduce. This can set up a terrible internal tension, and it can also drive a wedge into the relationship between parent and child, creating additional—and unnecessary—anguish for the infertile couple.

If the parents of an infertile couple feel guilty themselves, or take the blame on their own shoulders, the younger husband and wife often feel they have to contend not only with their own grief and worry, but that of their parents as well. This is an added burden they don't need. What may happen is that the younger couple withdraws from the older, creating distance and coldness when what everybody really needs at this point is warmth and support.

How do you handle your in-law problems connected to infertility? These tips can help:

For the couple: Let your parents know what is going on as early as possible. This will deflect the constant refrain, "When will we hear the good news?," which can be an ongoing reminder of your heartache. Tell them that this is a particularly hard time for you, that you are doing all you can to work it out, but that you need some space to do so. Let them know how much you hurt, and that you understand how hard it is for them to have to stand by and do nothing—but that it would be less upsetting to you if that was *exactly* what they did.

In addition, be very direct in assuring your in-laws that you are not rejecting *them*, but that you need to work this dilemma out for yourselves. Use "I" or "We" statements: "We love you, Mom and Dad, and we want your love and support in return, and we need some privacy right now to get through this."

For the couple's parents: Once they've shared the news of their problem with you, give your children a vacation from information-sharing. Assure them that you understand how painful the situation is, how intrusive the medical tests, how sad the failure month after month. This has to be a time when they don't feel compelled to share every last detail of every last test. Also, refrain from offering pseudomedical tidbits on how Margie down the street tried to get pregnant for six years, then quit her job and got pregnant right away; or how Pam in your office couldn't conceive for years, until she began taking Vitamin E three times a day. Your son and daughter-in-law don't want to hear it. Stories of all the women you know who tried a particular remedy and became pregnant immediately are hurtful rather than helpful.

As stressful and dismaying as this period may be, it can also bring in-laws together, as they rally to support each other. An understanding manner and a loving shoulder will be well appreciated (and long remembered) by the couple anguishing over the baby they so desperately want.

Delivering the News

Finally, the moment you—and your parents and *his* parents—have been waiting for! The baby is due in the spring, and it's time to tell the world. My advice is, forget the world and tell the grandparents-to-be first. Don't let them hear about the impending event from someone else before they hear it from you; getting that sort of news secondhand can lead to resentment and bitterness.

My friend Sam, a widower, was in Israel recently, where he had a warm and lovely visit with his daughter-in-law's parents in Tel Aviv. As he was leaving their apartment, the mother embraced Sam and said she'd see him in the United States in October, and looked forward to the visit in the fall.

Back home in Boston, Sam's son and daughter-in-law filled in the missing piece: They were expecting a baby in October. Fortunately, Sam was so filled with joy at the news he been waiting for during the past two years that his excitement overcame any resentment that his son's in-laws had got the announcement first—and long distance at that. He admitted, though, a certain chagrin that he'd had to play catch-up in the news department, and he acknowledged that he'd have been happier to have been told a little sooner—at least at the same time as his son's in-laws.

Make sure you approach this business of sharing good news with an eye toward fairness and equality. You might make a small dinner party out of it, toasting the coming event with champagne as you tell your parents and his that they're about to enter that hallowed and honored territory of grandparenthood.

THE NAME GAME

As the pregnancy progresses, it's usually a good time to convene a casual family meeting and talk about mutual expectations: What does each generation hope for and expect from the other? First-time parents and grandparents come to their new roles with little preparation for the nitty-gritty. Both generations may have thought wistfully and dreamily about a soft and cuddly baby in a lacy white christening gown, who never screamed for a two o'clock feeding or threw up on grandfather's jaunty blue silk tie. Right from the start it's helpful for everyone to define—out loud and clearly, using as many "I" statements as possible—what they expect from the other.

Will the grandparents baby-sit when they're called on? Will the parents be willing to hear (and heed) advice on feeding, clothing, and bathing the baby from people who have been there before? Will the grandparents have access to the new bundle of joy, or will they have to fight their way through protective parents? These are the types of issues that can be addressed now, before patterns of behavior become firmly entrenched and resentments are allowed to build up.

The name game should also come up now, and a family meeting is an ideal place to begin. The naming of a child is always seen as an honor in our society; how it is awarded and who gets it can make or break a relationship. Grandparents who have their heart set on a William Trent Halsey Hollingsworth III only to greet a Max nine months down the road are going to carry some heavy feelings of betrayal around with them . . . unless they've been tactfully and caringly prepped by Max's mommy and daddy in the months before the name becomes a reality.

The person who has the right to name a child often wields the power in a relationship. You'll realize as you head into your ninth month, still haggling over Linda Ellen or Ellen Linda, that there's much more to selecting a name than opening up a book of lists, closing your eyes, and running your finger down the right-hand column.

As a grandparent-to-be, you may feel that you have a lot at stake here. You may want desperately to honor a deceased mother or father by naming an heir after her or him. Or you may secretly feel that your own name should be the one bestowed on the new baby, as a symbol of ongoing history and respect.

Honesty and flexibility on everyone's part go a long way toward smoothing—or even avoiding—ruffled feathers at this point. You may firmly believe that your parents are holding out for that W.T.H. Hollingsworth III, only to be pleasantly surprised, once you discuss it, that the name is not as important to them as you'd imagined. Or you might not have realized how important it is to your wife's parents that their granddaughter be named after the family matriarch. Now's the time to find that out, not later, when the birth certificate is already registered at city hall.

A word to grandparents-to-be who use money or gifts to win over the parents-to-be in the name game: Don't. Nothing could be more underhanded. "I'll buy the nursery if you'll use 'Beverly Josephine' " may get you a little Beverly Josephine running around in a few months, but you'll also have a set of parents who resent your manipulation.

Clearly, choosing baby names can be dangerous to the health of your relationship with your in-law, but with tact, open expression, and understanding, it can also be fun and exciting.

Take My Advice... Please

A family meeting during early pregnancy is a wonderful time to talk about naming, and it's also an appropriate time to work out whose advice is going to prevail as the pregnancy progresses, and later, when the baby makes his or her appearance. Whose opinion will hold sway—the younger generation's, the older generation's, or the doctor's? If you're expecting a baby, you've probably already noticed that it's not unusual for everyone to chime in with an opinion, and that you feel confused, bewildered, and overwhelmed. "I remember when I was carrying you, Linda, the doctor said I should nap every afternoon and not do any heavy exercise," your mother might say. "Nonsense, Linda," rebuts your mother-in-law, "I played tennis and swam ten laps a day until the day Raymond was born." Whose advice do you trust? And how can you defuse this potentially explosive situation?

A few carefully chosen sentences at this point to either your mother or your mother-in-law can do wonders to ease this situation. "Mom," you might say, "I feel most comfortable about doing what the doctor tells me to do, but Ray and I appreciate your input, and value what you have to say."

The birth itself, and the way you plan to deliver, may also be a source of conflict, as younger mothers- and fathers-to-be explore such options as birthing rooms and midwife deliveries. In the eyes of the older generation, these "newfangled ways" can pose a threat to the well-being of the grandchild on whom they've pinned so many hopes—and to the well-being of the mother herself.

You, as the mother-to-be, have to be sensitive to these fears, and help your parents and your husband's parents accept your plans and respect your desires by explaining them openly and caringly. Talking it all out early in the pregnancy allows the older generation to know what to expect, and you can allay their apprehensions with reports from medical experts citing the safety of the birth method you've chosen.

Reality Checking Again

For both the expectant parents and the expectant grandparents, talking to others in the same situation will help you put your emotions into perspective and get a handle on how grounded in reality your expectations and fears are. If you're pregnant, you might chat with friends who have recently had babies of their own to see how they've tackled the thorny grandparent issues. Did they come to some agreement that Jake's parents would watch the baby every Saturday night when Jake and Lana went out? If so, how did they negotiate the deal? If you're about to become a grandmother or grandfather, you can seek out your peers who have already entered the club, and ask them for any secrets they might share.

This is also a time to tune in to any cultural factors that will come into play down the road. In some cultures—Middle Eastern and Mediterranean societies, for example—the role of the grandparent is more hands-on than it is in the West. Here in the United States, the role of the grandparent is undergoing monumental changes as the older generation gets younger—literally. Today, women at seventy are doing things that years ago only women in their fifties and sixties were active and fit enough to do: playing tennis, swimming laps, going back to college, working full time. Grandparents today are often active members of the work force, with very full social lives and less time to devote to the traditional role of "elder statesman." This can create conflicts as the new parents remember their *own* nurturing (and available) grandparents, and the impact they had on each other's lives.

Gwen, a striking woman with close-cropped hair, has run into this situation. Her mother-in-law, Lorraine, works full time as a computer troubleshooter, and has limited time to spend with her eighteen-month-old granddaughter, Ashley. Lorraine leaves the house at 7 A.M., and doesn't return home some nights until eight. Then she's too tried to face an evening of caring for a toddler. Although the older woman adores the child—and Gwen realizes this on an intellectual level—the new mother can't help feeling that Lorraine is ignoring Ashley, a suspicion she shares with her husband, Ronald.

The notion is upsetting to the young father. If his mother is rejecting his baby girl, Ronald reasons, she's rejecting *him* also.

What can you do if you share Ronald and Gwen's desire for a more participatory grandma, one who fits the old image of the plump, aproned woman whose hands were covered with flour and whose kitchen always smelled of cinnamon and cloves? You can realize that for many women this role doesn't fit either their personalities or their lifestyles.

That doesn't mean that the love and the warmth and the closeness can't be there. Look for opportunities to create those emotions: If Grandma is tied up during the week, take full advantage of weekends to be together. If she's exhausted after a long day at the office, invite her to your house for a nice home-cooked dinner and a chance to cuddle with her grandchild without fussing in the kitchen. If her working conditions permit, bring the baby to her at lunchtime and let her revel in her colleagues' oohs and ahs when she proudly shows off her grandchild.

If you're the grandmother, talk over your daughter-in-law's concerns openly and honestly, and be willing to be as flexible as possible with your time. Call her home during a coffee break just to ask, "How's that special grandson of mine doing? I miss holding him." Suggest that you'd love to have him to yourself one day every other weekend. If this suits you, the arrangement will give the new parents some desperately needed time off, and it will help you cement a bond with your grandchild, especially if this becomes a tradition for just the two of you over the ensuing years.

Taking Stock Early On

The level of involvement of parents and in-laws during the pregnancy is often a yardstick for how involved they will be once the baby arrives. If you feel that your mother-in-law is *too* wrapped up in your pregnancy—to the point where she bugs you with three or four phone calls a day to remind you to take your iron pills—or that she is too distant, now is the time, *before* the baby comes, to air your feelings. "I feel sad that you never asked me what the obstetrician said at my last visit," you might say. "Would you like to hear now? I'd like to share it with you." It's never too early to work toward openness and honesty in a relationship, and this type of message lets your mother-in-law know how much involvement you're comfortable with.

This can become especially crucial later on, after the baby arrives on the scene and feelings are heightened, raw, and new. Often a frank and open exchange of fears and/or expectations can avert hard feelings down the road.

Mary Anne, a sturdy-looking redhead who still carried some of the weight she had gained during her pregnancy, was deeply troubled that her mother-in-law, Anita, didn't want anything to do with her three-month-old grandson, Zachary. Anita would gaze lovingly at the gurgling baby, tickle his tummy, and coo at him, but pick him up? Never.

"It's as though she couldn't care less for Zack," Mary Anne said to her husband, Donald. What never occurred to either of them was that the older woman might be *afraid* to pick up Zachary. "No way," Mary Anne scoffed when I suggested this to her. "My mother-in-law had three children of her own; you'd think she'd be able to pick up *mine.*"

Anita was not a young woman, though, and many winters had passed since she'd last cradled an infant. I reminded Mary Anne of this, and suggested to her that Donald's mother might be feeling doubts about her ability to care for Zachary, maybe even harboring the secret fear that she would drop the baby if she picked him up. After our talk, Mary Anne sat down with her mother-in-law and gently retaught her the skills that had become rusty from disuse—how to scoop up the baby, how to support his head and neck with her forearm. Lo and behold: Anita remembered the old ways, and soon began to feel more at ease with carrying her tiny grandson throughout her house and garden.

A little early openness on the part of both Mary Anne and Anita might have avoided the bitterness and uncertainty that had taken hold, and saved both women months of anguish. You can't assume that because your mother-in-law raised six children, she'll feel as comfortable with yours. Although a woman might have had children twenty or thirty years ago, she may not feel comfortable about caring for an infant today. Sometimes an older woman fears she won't be able to learn how to work those darned disposable bottles, and the tapes on plastic diapers. Have patience with the new grandmother and grandfather—those skills may be rusty, but with a little bit of polish they'll shine once more.

Whose Baby Is It, Anyway?

The birth of a child and the baby's immediate first few weeks can be a time when new bonds form between the generations—or it can be a time when negative habits become ingrained and set in stone. If you're a new grandmom, you might see your son or daughter's infant child as an extension of yourself, and become overly involved right from the start. It's hard to keep your perspective when you think your son and daughter-in-law are not doing the type of job you could do yourself. In your passionate love for that tiny bundle, you might forget completely that the child is not yours, and try to wrest control from the rightful owner.

Ironically, the tendency of many women today to establish careers before starting a family can make this an even more irresistible option for you. Especially if this is her first child, a new mother is likely to have had a social network that was primarily job-related. When she leaves work to deliver her child, she leaves behind not only her colleagues and supervisors, but also her friends and her de facto support system. So now she's home with a helpless infant who doesn't want to talk with her about spreadsheets and the prime interest rate, or about Fred-down-the-hall's pending divorce. Instead, she's faced with a dizzying array of disposable diapers, disposable bottles, infant seats, cribs, tiny T-shirts that need constant washing, and a human being who can't be programmed like a computer. She's ripe for a takeover bid by an overly anxious grandmother.

Claudia was a new mom who lived six blocks away from Victoria, her widowed mother-in-law. Claudia looked forward to the first few months after the birth of her son, Jeffrey, as a time to get to know her husband's mother better. For the first four years of her marriage to Lenny, the younger woman had worked full time managing a fast-food restaurant; now she had the time she'd lacked to spend time with Victoria, and she was ready—eager, even—to forge a stronger bond. She envisioned Victoria coming over once or twice a week for tea and a chat; maybe she'd even get a chance toward the end of the visit to run out and pick up a few things at the supermarket while Grandma watched Jeffrey. That way Victoria and her grandson would be able to bond, also.

"So much for *that* daydream," an embittered Claudia said. "Victoria responded to my overtures by coming in and completely taking over! It wasn't as though Lenny hadn't warned me—he'd frequently complained about his mother's overinvolvement in his life. She calls him at the office every day, and before we were married, she expected him to stop by to see her three or four times a week. After Jeffrey was born, I got a first hand look at what Lenny was going through!"

Victoria threw herself into grandparenting with a passion. She took it upon herself to buy Jeffrey the kind of sleepers and snowsuits *she* liked, the kind of baby food *she* thought most nutritious.

She showed up at Claudia's door twice a week, then three times, then daily, announcing that she'd come to put Jeffrey in for his nap, read him a story, give him a bath.

Like a typical first-time mother, Claudia was feeling pretty insecure about her ability to care for this ten-pound bundle of squalling infant. She'd never before needed parenting skills, and she felt as though she was in over her head. So at first she welcomed Victoria's help and suggestions.

For her part, Lenny's mother sensed this weakness and used it to her advantage. With barbed comments and criticism ("You've let him stay in that wet diaper too long; look, now he's gotten diaper rash. . . ."), she fostered more and more self-doubt in Claudia and carved out more and more territory for herself. Pretty soon she was taking over the bulk of Jeffrey's rearing, and Claudia was watching helplessly from the sidelines as it happened.

The situation was dangerously close to destroying the young couple's marriage. Lenny was upset and exasperated to find his mother in the house every afternoon when he came home from work, and his wife was feeling guilty and depressed over her loss of control of her home, her baby, her marriage . . . her life.

What can you do if you find yourself in Claudia's situation? The first thing might be to build up some confidence in your abilities as a mother by seeking out new contact with other first-time mothers through playgroups, church-supported activities, or bulletin boards in supermarkets and other outlets. By chatting with other "novice" moms, you may start to establish a better sense of your own abilities and realize that your skills are sounder than you might have thought.

In Claudia's case, the constant climate of criticism had badly damaged her already-shaky feelings of self-worth as a mother. Getting together with others in the same boat, comparing notes about feeding, diapering, and bathing, would have allowed her to see that other young women shared her doubts but were coping with them.

Once you've started to feel better about yourself and your parenting abilities, you can address the next problem: disengaging an overly involved grandmother from her infant grandson. With Claudia, her first line of defense was Lenny, a natural ally since he, too, was feeling overwhelmed by his mother's take-charge approach.

By supporting Claudia in front of his mother with simple statements of agreement—"I think Claudia's right; the baby is warm enough"—the young husband built up Claudia's self-image and presented a united front to his mother. This, in turn, not only strengthened the couple's own relationship, but also reinforced in Victoria's mind the fact that they wanted to make *their own* decisions about their baby.

In addition to enlisting your husband's help, your next step would be to lay out a strategy that is nonconfrontational but firm and gentle. As each incident arises, respond politely but firmly to your mother-in-law's decrees: "Mom, I've already decided that Laurie will have peas and carrots today, not strained squash." "No, I don't think the yellow sweater is too light for today; it's not really that cold out." If your mother-in-law protests or tries to intimidate you, you can turn to your next ally: your pediatrician. "I checked with Dr. Lewis, and he said that if Elissa has a fever, I should put her to bed wearing a T-shirt and diaper. No, he said she doesn't need that heavy sleeper."

Realize that this process may take months—it took that long to develop, didn't it? Eventually your mother-in-law will back off as she begins to see you as more competent, more in charge. Then you might suggest to her—again, with a firm but loving tone—that she not come by quite so frequently. Reinforce this request by absenting yourself from the house and plugging more and more into the new social network you've established. If she's wise, she'll realize that if she doesn't give you and her son some space to raise your child yourself, she runs the serious risk of losing you—and her grandchild, to boot.

Stirring Up Old Conflicts

The birth of a first child, and that child's early years, can be a pivotal time in the life cycle of an intermarried couple, stirring up old emotions and conflicts with in-laws long thought buried. Many is the Christian grandfather who is shocked to learn that his new grandson is going to be raised as a Jew, or the Jewish grandmother who confronts the unwelcome news that her granddaughter will be enrolled in a Catholic parochial school for catechism lessons. All the issues you'd thought had been settled before the wedding are suddenly reawakened, all the pain rushes back in.

Betty, a devout Episcopalian who had raised her daughter Cheryl with a love and respect for her church, wasn't happy when Cheryl married David, a Jewish high school principal, in a civil ceremony. She had come to terms with the marriage, and had even begun to get along well with David, until the baby, Brandon was born—and a bris, or a ritual circumcision, was scheduled. Now, Betty felt as though she was in mourning; first she "lost" her daughter, now she had "lost" her grandson as well. She felt that her values were being rejected—that she herself was being rejected. Although she went to the circumcision ceremony and mingled with the guests, she felt lonely, uncomfortable, and ignored.

I urged Betty to talk over her feelings with Cheryl, to tell her daughter of her fears that her grandson would be brought up in a religion alien to hers. I encouraged her to learn a little about Judaism's customs and beliefs, so she would be on firmer ground when the youngster talked to her of his experiences. I reassured her that the couple's choice of religious upbringing for Brandon was not a renunciation of Betty and her values, but rather a decision based on their own spiritual and emotional needs. I suggested that she go to her own clergyman, who was sympathetic and understanding, as another source of comfort. You can do the same.

Moving In Again

Your husband has been one of the fifty workers let go in the company's latest consolidation move, and the rent's due next week but there's no money coming in. Your wife's been transferred to her dream job in San Diego, but it'll be a while until you can sell your house in Boston, get your affairs in order, and join her out there with the kids. The interim solution for both these situations: moving in—temporarily, you hope and pray—with the in-laws.

You may have done it before, and it worked out well. It can work out well again, but you have to know this: It's different with a child. Or children. The reasons may be the same—economic reversal, moving from one house to another and needing a short-term resting place—but the complications kids add make the proposition more fraught with dangers.

What comes up most are issues of discipline and expectations. How often will the grandparents baby-sit while the parents are out looking for work? Whose rules apply when it comes to setting curfews and doling out punishments? If Grandpa wants to give little Sandra two cookies after dinner and Mom insists on fruit, who prevails? Kids aren't dumb; they very quickly learn to pit one adult against another. Then you lose, your in-law loses, the children ultimately lose, and everybody feels resentment and frustration.

The solution here is to become allies rather than antagonists.

Arguing or countercommanding in front of the children just encourages their manipulation. Instead, support the other adult but be firm about your own rules: "I know Grandpa said you could have two cookies, but you know our rules about after-dinner snacks." At another time, outside of hearing range of the children, you can privately and politely explain your position to your father-in-law, encouraging him to honor your rule about no junk food between meals.

As a mother, you certainly don't have to lose your control over your children if you're living with in-laws. Setting rules ahead of time, compromising as much as possible—"Okay, my kids won't leave their toys in the foyer; how about if you remove all the glass vases from the living room so they won't break if the kids get a little rambunctious?"—can make the process as painless as possible.

These questions of authority also plague the grandparents. It's best to leave discipline to the parents, and tell them you are doing so.

All parties who are struggling to find their proper roles in this new extended family should keep in mind, too, that there's an added bonus to living together under one roof. Grandparent and grandchild might forge a bond that never would have existed if the two families had not had this chance to live together. Years from now, your kids may look back with joy and deep satisfaction at having had a loving grandfather or grandmother so close at hand as they struggled through the challenges of growing up.

"The Grandparent Trap?"

"Dear Ann Landers: I'm sending this with no comment. I'd like to see it in print. Please sign me—a Burlington, Vt. Grandma." The letter followed:

"I'm caught in the grandparent trap.

"I'm the grandchildren's cook. If I didn't do it, they would be eating junk.

"I'm the laundress. If I didn't wash their clothes, they'd be filthy.

"I'm the barber. If I didn't do it, they'd look like ragamuffins.

"I'm the cleaning lady. If I didn't do it, their home would look like a tornado hit it.

"I'm the sewing lady. My daughters are too lazy. If I didn't make the children's clothes, they would be wearing rags.

"I'm the religion teacher. If I didn't do it, my grandchildren would be atheists.

"I'm my grandchildren's ear. Their parents are too busy to listen.

"I'm the one who reminds them of their appointments. They have the habit of forgetting everything.

"I teach the grandchildren manners. If I didn't, they would act like barbarians.

"I'm the referee. There is always someone fighting. Their parents never hear a thing.

"I'm the social worker. They all go for counseling, but they only get pampered. I'm the only one who lays it on the line.

"I am old, sickly and not well-educated. My children, on the other hand, are young, healthy and well-educated. How come I have all this common sense and they don't have any?"

The letter to syndicated advice columnist Ann Landers published in the *Philadelphia Inquirer*, July 16, 1989 did not say whether this long-suffering woman lived with her grandchildren or if she just came over after school to watch them. It didn't say whether her strong participation had been solicited by the children's parents—or whether it was even welcome. I would dearly love to hear the daughter's (or daughter-in-law's) version of this situation. If a daughter-in-law wrote such a letter, I think it would go something like this:

"Dear Ann Landers: I work full time outside the home, and am trying to juggle all the responsibilities of pursuing a career, parenting, being a good daughter and daughter-in-law. My mother-in-law is constantly on my back about my 'failures' as a mother, and as a person. She thinks I'm demanding, ungrateful, a poor housekeeper, and a lousy parent. Whenever I ask her to help me out in some way—pick up the kids after school, run my son to the pediatrician—she'll do it, but for a price. That price is nagging. I'm feeling a lot of tension, pressure, and guilt. Signed, Beleaguered Daughter-in-Law."

Who's right it this scenario? Both parties—and neither.

Burlington Grandma, you've earned the right to look forward to spending time with grandchildren not as a surrogate mother but as a beloved grandmother. I'm afraid, though, that you may be sabotaging yourself by being overly critical, harping on differences in parenting styles and lifestyles, and not recognizing that there are many ways of doing things that are not necessarily worse than yours . . . just different.

For example, you complain about your grandchildren's nutrition. You may have turned out the traditional meat/potato/ vegetable dinners for your family night after night, and now you watch as your daughter-in-law orders in pizza and Chinese food. That doesn't mean your grandchildren are not getting a balanced diet—or that your daughter-in-law is not a good mother. You may be implying that because she works, your daughter-in-law is "too busy" to spend time with her children. Years ago, women in your generation were financially able to live well on one salary; today it just as frequently takes two incomes to balance the budget at the end of the month. Even those women who choose to work outside the home for personal reasons have every right to do so. Again, there's a difference in styles—not necessarily in quality. If you constantly hold up "your way" as the only way or as the best way, you're creating an unhealthy competition between yourself and your daughter-in-law over who is the better parent. It's a competition neither one of you can win.

Now, Burlington Grandma, what if your gripes are legitimate ones? What if your granddaughter acts like an uncivilized terror at restaurants, picking up food with her fingers and barking orders to the waiter? Then you have every right to talk to her parents—*both* parents, not just singling out her mother for your criticism—in a polite, tactful way. Rather than "Charlotte acts like a monster when I take her out to dinner; you must not have taught her any manners," a series of "I" statements directed to both mother and father would be helpful.

You might approach it like this: "I'm concerned when Charlotte eats out with me, she doesn't seem to know how to behave. I wonder how she is when she goes out with you." This is not an attack, it's not confrontational, and it allows you to launch a discussion to work together to solve the problem.

It seems to me, Grandma, that you also have to do some thinking about your gripes and about the level of participation with which your feel comfortable. If you feel put-upon by doing the laundry—don't do it. You'll have to balance your priorities here; if you really hate the way your grandchildren look, then you'll either continue washing their clothes, or you'll swallow your displeasure over the kids' appearance. Either way, do it gracefully—or not at all.

Now, on to you, Beleaguered Daughter-in-Law. Believe it or not, your mother-in-law's criticisms may not be so far out; her advice may even be helpful. Often, when you're overwhelmed by balancing all the roles, an objective word from someone who's looking on can give you a new perspective. There may be gold in all that dross; it's a matter of sifting through all of it and gleaning what you need. Your mother-in-law may have a better way of organizing the laundry, planning menus, or keeping your appointments straight—you won't know unless you open your mind to her suggestions.

All too often, in-law advice sounds like a criticism or a put-down. What you must do is separate the message from the way it is delivered. If your mother-in-law openly scorns your daughter's table manners, for example, you might take the older woman aside and say, "Mom, I feel that you are accusing me of something. I'm willing to discuss Charlotte's behavior, but I'd rather you didn't attack me personally." That way, you're encouraging your husband's mother to share her observations in a civilized manner.

If the grandparental harping goes on and on, I emphasize to my clients, "You are the parents, you have a right to say, '*Stop!* We don't want to hear it.' "

At this point, it's imperative for couples to work together on a game plan for approaching the intrusive in-laws. Your husband can be the one to talk to his mother—parents tend to take criticism better from their children than from their in-laws, research has shown. Even if your husband doesn't feel the brunt of the criticism as keenly, even if he shares some of his mother's concerns, it is his role to deflect the barrage of gripes coming at you, his wife. Again, with "I" statements: "I love you, Mother, but I would prefer that you keep your criticism to yourself. I recognize your concern, but Marge and I are the parents, and we'll take care of the situation." It all goes back to learning to set limits, and then enforcing those limits. All parties will feel more comfortable once the boundaries are clearly enunciated—with love, tact, and understanding.

What if your husband refuses to confront his mother? Obviously, your approach will be more effective if you work together, but if he is reluctant to engage in battle, or if he feels as though the issue is not that important, you will have to confront your mother-in-law yourself.

When Baby Makes ... Bonds

The birth of a baby doesn't have to be a source of trauma between in-laws. Sometimes, when the struggles surrounding wedding plans have created rifts and tensions, the coming of an infant works to bring the extended families together as one. They're not *his* parents and *her* parents anymore, but rather they're the baby's grandparents. Remember the old joke—what do the grandparents and the child have in common? Both have the same enemy: *Mom!*

You'll often be surprised to realize, as you watch your own infant grow and struggle toward independence, that it's not as easy as you might have thought to be a parent. On the contrary, it's one of the most difficult and demanding assignments you will ever have in your life. With that dawning realization can come admiration for the job your own parents or parents-in-law did, and an understanding of the challenges they faced with you and your husband when *you* were children.

Similarly, as new grandparents watch their children feel their way through the trials of early parenthood, they may marvel at the difficulties facing parents today and feel proud of the job they're doing against all odds. From this admiration, too, comes closeness and trust.

Summing Up

Gradually, you have to come to recognize that there are some things about your in-laws that you might not like but can't change. For example, your daughter-in-law's standards of housekeeping are not up to yours or your father-in-law persists in pushing unwanted advice on you. You are beginning to accept reality and adjusting to what *is*, not what you dreamed *might* be.

In many ways, what makes the relationships move forward at this point is this very acceptance—your acceptance of your in-laws, their acceptance of you. This new sense of understanding and maturity will serve you well as you move into the middle years of your marriage.

CHAPTER FIVE

The Middle Years

Mother of Another

You were just the mother of another
Until my union with your son.
And as our family begins to grow
I can appreciate all the work you've done.
We join together as a group
To share our precious gifts.
I know that we can come to you
If we need a lift.
Please be assured I treasure him
And will do the best I can.
You used to nurture the little boy
Now I champion the man.

—ANONYMOUS

This verse was being cross-stitched by Dottie, who was sitting in the audience of one of my in-law seminars, her needle flashing in and out of the wall-hanging on which she was working so intently. When I admired her handiwork and asked about the verse she had chosen, she said she had gotten it from a magazine. She was making this gift for her mother-in-law, she said, because the two women were entering a very special new phase of their relationship. In the beginning, Dottie said, she'd had a hard time accepting the older woman, but when she became a parent herself, she began to appreciate Loretta more.

When Dottie's daughter, Annie, was diagnosed with leukemia, Loretta was a source of comfort and strength to the whole family, always available to run Annie to the doctor, and helping out those nights when Dottie was just too exhausted to provide the intense care a dying child needs.

"It's been two years now since Annie died, and Loretta has always been there for me, whether it's as a shoulder to cry on or a hand when just the idea of cooking dinner is too overwhelming," said Dottie, who'd come to the workshop that night to keep a friend company. "She still has her quirks that get on my nerves—I can't stand it when she constantly adjusts my scarf or turns down the collar on my blouse—but I've come to respect her strengths and admire her abilities. My mother-in-law is truly a special lady."

It took a family tragedy for Dottie and Loretta to reach this plateau in their relationship, but even without upheaval and crisis, many in-laws find that the coming of marriage's middle years brings warmth, respect, and understanding where once tension and animosity may have ruled. Like Dottie, you may realize that even though some issues have not fully resolved themselves, there are positive aspects of the relationship that have allowed you to look at each other as people, not just as "the other woman."

At this point in your marriage your children are probably of school age and you've adjusted to being a family of more than two people. Chances are you have your own home or apartment, are fairly well established in your career, and are financially independent. The all-consuming issues of early marriage have been put to rest and you've learned to coexist with your spouse, appreciating his strengths and tolerating his weaknesses—and he yours.

So it is with your in-laws, too. You've made your peace over which family will have you for Christmas and which for Easter; over the fact that you *hate* it when she drops in unannounced at the dinner hour, so now she sometimes calls first; over the fact that she doesn't cook a pot roast the way you always did, but hers is pretty good, anyway. You've realized that the relationship does for the most part balance itself out—and that, somewhere along the way, you stopped being so angry at her and maybe even began to enjoy her.

These "middle ages" of a marriage, like the pivotal first few months after the wedding, are an ideal time to stop and take stock of where you are—and where you should be. Get a piece of paper and a pencil, and take the following quiz, which is designed to help you rate the relationship with your in-laws and to put your ongoing dealings with each other into perspective.

Read each of the following statements and, using a number from zero to 100, rate your in-law and how he/she measures up. Be honest with yourself, and look at the overall relationship rather than focusing on the argument you and your daughter-in-law might have had last night over whether your granddaughter should be allowed to stay out until midnight, or you and your mother-in-law had over her reading your mail.

How to assign the number? Think of zero as the worst-possible-case scenario. When you consider, for example, "How much do you trust your in-law?," you'd probably say zero if you've caught her stealing money from your purse, if you've heard her lying to her husband, and if you've seen her in a compromising position with another man. On the other hand, if she has never said an untrue word to you, if you've heard her tell a store clerk that she undercharged her for the paper towels, if you would trust her with your life, go for the 100.

Ready? Go.

Rating the Relationship

1. How well does she listen to you?
   0 100
2. How open-minded is she in your dealings with each other?
   0 100
3. How does your relationship compare to what you thought it would be like?
   0 100
4. How much do you like spending time with her?
   0 100
5. How hard have you tried to make this relationship work well?
   0 100
6. How hard has she tried to make this relationship work well?
   0 100
7. How honest have you been with her?
   0 100
8. How honest has she been with you?
   0 100
9. How willing is she to share of herself and her feelings?
   0 100
10. How much do you trust her?
   0 100
11. How much fun do you have when you're with her?
   0 100

12. How frequently do you find areas of common interest?
    0 100
13. How much do you like her as a person?
    0 100

SCORING: This is not the kind of quiz in which you add up the scores and get a magic number to rate your relationship. Instead, look over each question separately and consider each number as a percentage. For example, say you answered 30 for the question, "How frequently do you find areas of common interest?" Now interpret that to mean that 30 percent of the time your interests intersect. At least 30 percent of the time, then, you have things in common: You both enjoy bowling, romance novels, and movies from the thirties and forties, for example. Considering your answer in this light gives you a chance to look at how much you share, rather than focusing on how vast the differences between you are.

As you examine each question, and rate each in terms of a percentage, you will see some patterns emerging. You also, I hope, will begin to see some of the positive aspects of the other person.

Again, be honest with yourself. If you write down only zero percents, ask yourself this: How did the man I cherish and respect come from a parent who has absolutely no redeeming qualities? Likewise, if your daughter-in-law gets a low score, reflect on how it is that the son you brought up to be a mature, responsible man with solid judgment can be the same man who loves and respects a woman so bereft of positive characteristics? You may need to look again at those numbers. I think you will find that you may be judging your in-law or even yourself too harshly.

The business of the middle years of marriage is to come to terms with problems that have continued to plague your relationship with your in-laws, addressing the longstanding issues that may have stood in the way of making peace. It's also time to locate those "time bombs" that exist in any marriage, and work to defuse them. Finally, it's time to express your appreciation for your in-laws in ways that can help your relationship grow and flourish.

Healing Old Wounds

Rachel, a quiet-voiced receptionist with curly brown hair, had dreamed of the perfect wedding since she was a child. Now, ten years after she and Jordan had exchanged vows, she was still carrying around a lot of bitterness and resentment, all directed at Jordan's mother, Rita. Why? Because the dress Rita had chosen to wear for her son's nuptials, the dress in which she walked down the aisle, the dress she wore on the day all of Rachel's dreams came true—was black. Pitch black. As in funeral.

"I couldn't believe it when she showed up at the church," Rachel said a decade later, the anger still not far from the surface. "All my friends said she had chosen black because she was in mourning for her son. I was embarrassed and mortified—and I've never forgiven her."

Long-ago slurs, whether intentional or unintentional, can drive a dwedge between the generations that continues to divide them long after the original incident. How often have you carried a grudge from an incident you can't even recall? These petty hatreds don't have to be chiseled in stone. The maturity that often accompanies the middle years of marriage can help you put a new perspective on ancient grievances.

Rachel, for example, had been lugging around her bitterness over the black-dress incident for so long that it had become a part of her. I suggested to her that she cast her mind back over the past decade and begin thinking of reasons Rita might have had for this monumental "insult" that set their relationship on such an unpleasant course. While reconstructing the time period, Rachel eventually remembered that her mother-in-law had had a figure problem—Rita still carried too much weight in the nether regions—and that she had probably looked to the black dress to minimize her flaws.

It didn't happen overnight, but finding other interpretations of an event that had plagued her for ten years helped Rachel cut through the undercurrent of tension and hostility that was always present when the two women came together. This new view helped Rachel let go of her anger.

As we enter our middle years, we tend to become less self-involved because we recognize and come to accept our own foibles. The younger people are, the more self-centered they tend to be. That's human nature. The teenager with the pimple on her nose agonizes that she's wearing a neon light in the middle of her face, until she gets older and realizes that not everyone is staring at her and that people have problems of their own with which they are preoccupied. In the middle years, you may find your perspective is broader; that whereas once you defined yourself as the center of everyone's universe, now you're content to occupy one little corner of that universe.

Once Rachel reached that point in her maturity, it was easier for her to see her mother-in-law's choice of a black dress not as a slap in the face to *her*, but rather as a heavyset woman's best attempt to look sleek and attractive at her beloved son's wedding. With this new understanding came tolerance, and, eventually, affection.

Parent Versus Parent

What happens when the ancient animosities are not between you and your in-laws, but between your parents and his parents? This is a common occurrence, and often the hostility harks back to the period leading up to the wedding, when the two older couples' interests, styles, and agendas clashed.

Joyce's parents, the Regans, and Theo's parents, the Morgans, agreed that when the kids got married, they would have a reception immediately after the church wedding. The hotel room they had booked held two hundred people comfortably. Looking over their budget and their guest list, the bride's parents told the Morgans that they could invite seventy-five guests and that they, the Regans, were inviting ninety. Knowing the size of the room, the groom's parents felt they were getting unequal treatment. The wedding went on as planned, but a wedge had been driven into the relationship between the two sets of parents, and it went deeper over the years.

Every time the families came together, even at little Katie's birthday parties, there was tension and wrangling among the parents-in-law. Theo and Joyce found themselves in the extremely awkward and uncomfortable position of having to pacify both sets of parents without seeming to side with either. Occasions that should have been joyful were painful; even the grandchildren were caught in the crosscurrents of resentment.

What could you do as a younger couple embroiled in this kind of mess? First, remember that as uncomfortable as the situation may be, your parents are adults; it's not your job to rectify the situation or even go out of your way to keep them apart to prevent confrontations. What *is* your responsibility is always to let each set of parents know if the other is going to be at a party or holiday dinner. That leaves it up to them whether they wish to attend.

If outright fights do break out, you have to talk to each older couple separately, telling them how much their behavior is hurting the entire family—grandchildren included. No accusations. Just, "Dad and Mom, we love to get together with you and Joyce's parents, but when you insult them to their faces, we all get upset. Our family gatherings mean a lot to us, and we want to include everyone, so maybe you could try to put up with the Regans for one night every few months, okay?"

Remember, parents will take constructive criticism more readily from their own child than from that child's spouse. Therefore, each of you should approach *your own* parent separately and individually to try to resolve the animosity.

To the bickering older generation, I offer this advice: You don't have to have a wonderful relationship with your son's in-laws; you do have to do everything in your power to keep family get-togethers from turning into the verbal equivalent of a boxing match at Madison Square Garden. Obviously, there are going to be disagreements in parenting styles and lifestyles. Try to keep in mind that you will probably see these people only on special occasions, and that although there is no formal relationship that binds you, you are united by the love of your children—and your grandchildren. If you can cling to the thought that you will probably be together only four or five hours every few weeks, if that, then you can manage to be cordial and sociable. If not for yourselves, at least for the sake of your sons and daughters.

Time Bombs

Even if your parents and your husband's adore each other, there are occasions during the year when extended families are thrown together and must accommodate a wide range of needs, feelings, egos, and agendas. Sometimes these are events such as funerals, which carry their own built-in tensions; other times they are joyous and celebratory, but they still have the potential to perpetuate family rivalries or hostilities. Think of all the ways families come together in the course of a year:

1. Family reunions
2. Birthday parties
3. Christenings

4. Confirmations
5. Bar or bat mitzvahs
6. Graduations
7. Dance recitals
8. School plays
9. First communions
10. Wedding anniversaries
11. Engagement showers
12. Weddings
13. Births
14. Funerals
15. Sweet sixteen parties
16. Religious and secular holidays

Each one of these occasions carries unlimited potential for unpleasant encounters and hostility—or for satisfying encounters among family members who have learned to love and respect each other. If the tension between you and your in-laws is high, the gathering is tainted for everyone involved. Furthermore, at this point in your married life, the tension is often passed down to the children. Even if it's never verbalized, youngsters pick up on this type of stress, and will invariably side with the parents. Rarely will a child, who is still so dependent on Mommy and Daddy for sustenance, jeopardize that relationship by supporting Grandma or Grandpa in a conflict like this. So if you feel tense or anxious around your in-laws at family get-togethers, chances are young Mickey or Janie will feel the same—and chances are they will see Grandma or Grandpa as the "bad guys." Then the bonds between grandparent and grandchild are stretched or even broken, and everyone loses.

So it becomes especially important to plan these events—which almost always involve children as well as all extended family members—in such a way as to minimize tension and maximize enjoyment. I have a four-step plan you can use to make this happen.

How to Guarantee a Pleasant Family Party

1. Include your in-laws in some of the preliminary planning for an event such as a graduation party. It's not necessary to take all of their advice or agree with all of their input; just listening to them is a sign that you value their participation in the upcoming party. "Dad, I really like your idea of setting up a tent in the back yard for the guests. We'll look into it." "Mother, you're right, a white wine *would* go nicely with my chicken Kiev."
2. Designate a specific role for your in-laws to play in the festivies. Offer them some responsibilities, such as bringing a dessert, helping you greet the guests, or tending bar. In addition to giving you a hand, this arrangement also gives them a sense of worth and a feeling that they are an important part of what's going on.
3. Keep in mind your in-laws' specific needs. For example, if your father-in-law uses a wheelchair to get around, make sure ahead of time that there will be a place for him at the graduation ceremony where he won't be blocking an aisle but where he will be able to see the proceedings and watch his grandson pick up his diploma.
4. Introduce your in-laws to your friends and other relatives they may not have remembered or met until now. If they feel as though they are part of the celebration, they are less likely to find things to gripe about.

Although these middle years are ones of relative tranquillity—no pun intended—unresolved conflicts may continue to play themselves out on the field of your marriage. Often they concern the leftover issues of dashed expectations, unmet needs, and competition for time, attention, and affection.

Lois, a soft-spoken forty-two-year-old with a ready smile, had gone back to school after fifteen years at home as wife and mother. Before her marriage to Marshall, a sales rep for a furniture company, she had worked as a clerk in a library; now she was working toward a degree in social work. Her children, Candace, fourteen, and David, twelve, would be going off to college in a few years. By then, Lois figured, she'd be able to get a full-time job to help defray some of their expenses. Marshall was solidly behind her plan—and her.

Not so Marshall's mother, Kaye. Since Lois had started classes in the fall, the older woman had done nothing but complain—loudly and bitterly, to anyone who would listen—that Lois was neglecting Marshall and her kids. "My son looks tired," she would say. "*She's* forcing him to cook for himself and the kids, when she should be taking care of all of them. Why is she going back to school, anyway? Marshall makes a good living."

Lois took the badgering with good grace, but inside she was fuming. In addition, the constant criticism was eating away at her self-confidence and her sense of equilibrium. She was spending a great deal of energy juggling the needs of her family and the demands of her schoolwork; the last thing she needed was snide remarks from her mother-in-law, with whom she'd previously been on fairly good terms.

"How do I get Kaye off my back?" she wondered. "I don't want to hurt her feelings, but she's driving me crazy with this sniping. I spend so much time feeling upset and defensive, I can't concentrate on my classwork."

Because she was so overwhelmed, Lois was completely ignoring a natural ally: her husband, Marshall, who from the start had been supportive of his wife's decision to go back to college and who had stepped in willingly—even eagerly—to help out on the domestic front.

Your husband can play a vital role in smoothing the friction between you and your mother-in-law. He can stand up for you forcefully, letting his mother know that his needs are being met, that's he is happy with his wife, and that husband and wife arrived at their decisions jointly, with much adult discussion and weighing of pros and cons. He can also remind you that it's his *mother* who is being so disapproving, not *him*. His making this distinction will help you feel better about yourself and your marriage, and help you keep your perspective in the face of your mother-in-law's incessant harping.

You can also turn that griping around to your advantage. Instead of wasting good energy tuning it out, or responding in kind, you can pick up on the complaining and turn it back to its source—and you can do so to your advantage. Next time your mother-in-law complains that her son is not being properly cared for, seek out her help. "Yes, Mother, I agree Marshall is looking a little tired. We're all working really hard right now. I was wondering if next time you made a pan of lasagna, you might put an extra one up for us? That would sure make our lives easier one night when we both come home late."

If Kaye is responsive to this appeal for help, she can easily become part of the solution rather than part of the problem. In addition to getting a ready-made meal one night, you get a mother-in-law who feels needed, who feels she has contributed to her family's well-being, and who may very well feel less inclined to gripe if she's being included in some of the day-to-day running of her son's family.

What is often behind the bitterness and resentment many mother-in-laws express over their daughter-in-law's returning to school or work is a plain and simple feeling of abandonment. Before job or homework interfered, there may have been more frequent get-togethers, more relaxed family dinners, more telephone calls. With the younger woman so fully absorbed in her new role, these occasions can grow fewer and farther between. If you can get beyond the griping and read the emotion behind your mother-in-law's barrage, you might find her harping is caused by simple loneliness rather than condemnation. Giving her an important role to play—fixing the kids' dinner once or twice a week, attending a school play when you can't make it—goes a long way toward making her feel more a part of things.

On the other hand, you as the mother-in-law in this situation have to be sensitive to the needs of the younger generation. It's not easy balancing house/family/job/school. Instead of telling your daughter-in-law how to run her marriage, be direct and honest about your feelings. Tell both your son and his wife about your concerns, and talk them out as adults. You may be surprised to learn that rather than feeling neglected or overwhelmed, your son feels that he is playing an important role in his family. You might come to respect the juggling act your daughter-in-law is performing—and, in the process, come to respect your daughter-in-law. When honest emotions are shared, when fears and doubts are aired, a closer relationship can flourish.

I overheard a mother-in-law and daughter-in-law talking to one another as they were having coffee during a break in one of the workshops I was facilitating. The daughter-in-law was saying, "I used to think you were perfect, but when you began to show me you were human, I felt like I got to know you better and I was willing to let you know me better, too."

Her mother-in-law responded, "When I decided to show you my fears and doubts, it was because I was uncomfortable being placed on a pedestal. I was struggling with what to do with my life also. When I first talked to you about these things, you told me how you had gone through something similar—only at a younger age. I could see you were not so bad either."

Grumblings from (and about) Grandparents

If I had to isolate one source of ongoing stress at this midpoint of marriage, it would wear the kindly and wrinkled face of a grandparent. Both generations come to me with the old laments: "My mother-in-law is an absentee grandmother"; "My daughter-in-law won't listen when I talk to her about disciplining my youngest grandson, who's running wild in the streets." "My in-laws are constantly vying with my parents for my daughter's affections." As great a source of comfort and joy as grandchildren can be, they can also be the root of many an in-law conflict.

Anita is a full-time bookkeeper of thirty-five. Lately, she has been hearing an unwelcome litany from her father-in-law, Leonard, who lives about twenty minutes away by car. "I hardly ever see the boys," Leonard says frequently. "You bring them over only once a week, and then all they do is look at the clock till it's time to go. And when I come to your house, they're always outside playing."

Anita's sons, Neil, twelve, and Kyle, ten, complain to her that's it's "bor-r-r-ing" to visit their grandfather, that he spends a lot of time telling them not to touch this vase or that knick-knack, and that there's nothing to do at his house. They are normal, active boys who would rather spend their after-school hours playing soccer and hockey than visiting with an old man. Any attempt by Anita to encourage her sons to visit Leonard more often is met with a whiny, "Aw, Mom, do we hafta?"

Both generations in this conflict—no, make that all *three* generations—have to step back and see how a little understanding, planning, and good communication can make everyone happier.

Are you a grandparent whose grandchildren find any excuse to avoid a visit? Then you have to find out why. What does your granddaughter do when she comes over? What activities do you plan—if any? Often, something as simple as teaching her your favorite card game or having your grandchild bring over Monopoly or Parcheesi will make the hours speed by happily. If you're up to it, you could take your grandson roller-skating, and watch proudly as he whizzes around the rink with a grin on his face. What you have to recognize is that for a child, sitting around a house where he can't touch anything and where a grown-up is constantly reminding him to brush his hair, straighten his tie, and not to slurp his soup *is* "bor-r-r-ing." It was probably boring for *you* sixty years ago; it's equally boring for your grandchild today.

Moreover, you have to be willing to be flexible in arranging these visits, especially if your daughter and son-in-law work full time and find it hard to drive the children to you. Why not go to them—with a jigsaw puzzle you can work on together or a new word game to share? Or you can volunteer to drive crosstown to pick your grandkids up. It might take a little more effort on your part, but isn't it worth it?

Creativity is vital here. Rather than suffering in silence, sulking that your granddaughter never comes to see you, or putting pressure on your son-in-law to bring her over—be innovative. Find ways to make the connection with them that don't involve the busy parents. How about eliciting help from a friend who would love an afternoon at the zoo in exchange for providing transportation? There's no limit to the different ways you can make visits more frequent—and more pleasant for all.

Now a word to the parents. Don't be afraid to tell your in-law of your exceedingly tight schedule and even of the boys' reluctance to visit. Yes, you probably are wary of hurting feelings. That's understandable, but if you're totally honest, you and the grandparent can work toward making things better, rather than allowing him to stew about why Neil and Kyle aren't there—or blaming you for their absence in his life.

It's time, also, to have a talk with your children. In words geared to their age, encourage them to appreciate the unique bond between grandchild and grandparent. "Grandpa loves you in a very special way," you might begin. "There aren't any conditions on his love; it will be there whether you get an A on your report card or a C, whether you score the winning touchdown or fumble the ball."

One of the main differences between parental love and grandparental love is that parents feel responsible for the way their children behave, interpreting any misbehavior on the children's part as a reflection of how good (or *bad*) a parent they are. Grandparents don't have this particular stake in a grandchild's behavior; they can be more tolerant of tiny infractions of the rules or even major indiscretions.

Because of this special relationship, a grandparent can become a real ally, an advocate. Children learn this early: If Mom won't let me go to the roller rink with my friends because she thinks it's too dangerous, Nana can remind her that my dad was allowed to go when he was my age. Grandparents can fight for higher allowances, later curfews, more liberal attitudes toward friends—and can often win.

More important, you as a parent have to keep in mind that grandparents can be a source of living history for a child, a link with the generations that came before and a window offering a rare glimpse into their lives. Spending time with grandparents as frequently as possible can teach your sons and daughters that older people have much to offer in the way of experience and insight; that being elderly does not necessarily mean being frail or decrepit or unsound of mind. It's a very, very valuable lesson to learn.

Vying for Affection

It is Christmas at the Taylors. Grandma and Grandpa Taylor have promised seven-year-old Sammy a set of trains, with a trestle bridge and a moss-covered tunnel. Grandpa and Grandma Wharton, not to be outdone, are shopping for a Nintendo game, complete with all the cartridges. It's the same old story, Sammy's mother, Jean, says with a sigh. She doesn't want to tell her parents and her in-laws to stop giving gifts completely—that's not in the loving spirit of the holiday, and it's too drastic a solution, Jean believes. But something's got to give; with all the jockeying for Sammy's affection, the child is beginning to feel an inflated sense of importance, and he's also reached the unfortunate conclusion that love is something you can buy—with a set of trains or a Nintendo.

The intense competition is wreaking havoc on her marriage, also, Jean realizes. As the holidays near and she tenses for each round of gift-giving, she implores her husband, Barry: "Tell your mother to stop bringing so much stuff. It's not good for Sammy." "*My* mother?" comes Barry's response. "What about *your* mother? She's the one who started it!"

Jean should have set some limits on this situation years ago, when Sammy was a baby and her parents tried to outmaneuver her in-laws by providing the most elaborate layette and nursery furniture. As a new mother, she was overwhelmed with the demands of a crying infant, and she watched helplessly as one grandmother tried to outclass the other with Christian Dior diaper covers and Saks Fifth Avenue blankets. Fortunately, it's still not too late now to remedy the situation.

If you find yourself in this position, you can approach each set of grandparents and point out the problems their compulsive gift-giving is creating: "Mom, Dad, the role of grandparents is to give a child unconditional love. But trying to win him over with presents isn't doing anyone any good. We know you love Sammy and want the best for him, but trying to 'buy' him is harmful and just confuses him."

Grandparents should be aware that this jockeying to be number one is an easy trap to fall into. They should also be aware of how it looks to a child: The four adults whom he probably admires and adores most after his parents just keep plying him with gifts. After a while—a short while; kids aren't dumb—he'll begin to equate you with material things: "Oh, goody, Grandpa's coming. I bet he'll bring me a new bike." Or he'll start to play one set of grandparents against the other: "When Grandma Wharton comes over, she always brings me new videotapes," with the underlying message to the other grandmother, "Can you top this?"

Sure you can top it, but don't. Don't let yourself fall into that trap; it can diminish your grandchild's sense of self-esteem by making him feel like a prize to be "won," and it can engage you in a power struggle with his other grandparents that ultimately no one can win.

Instead, take every opportunity to play up the other grandparents in the child's eyes. Ask Sammy often how his other grandma and grandpa are doing and find something to praise about them—"Wasn't it fun when they took you to the zoo to see the white tiger there?" "Did Grandma Nelson teach you how to count so well? Isn't she smart?" Encourage him to talk about them by being interested when he mentions their outings together, and rather than being threatened by it, take pleasure in his excitement. This type of support can only enrich his family life as well as yours, as he learns that older people have much to offer—much more than all the dolls, games, bikes, and videos they can bring him.

Giving Credit Where It's Due

In order to put some of the long-standing problems behind you, to resolve simmering rivalries and lay old hatreds to rest, use these middle years of your marriage as a perfect time to find something about your in-laws to praise and appreciate. Remember, you didn't choose your daughter-in-law; your son did. There's no reason, though, why you can't share in his joy over the good things about her that make her special.

From the start, the bubbly, outgoing, and effervescent Audrey grated on her daughter-in-law's nerves. Sara was quieter, more reserved, almost shy. Not one to seek the limelight, she was appalled when Audrey almost took over Sara's bridal shower, directing the games, dishing out the food, and entertaining the guests with her loud jokes. In the decade since then, the younger woman had tried to distance herself from Audrey because of her distaste for her mother-in-law's brashness and brassiness.

Out to lunch with two close friends one afternoon, Sara complained about Audrey's boisterousness at a family dinner the night before. Her friend Amy stared at her in amazement. "I always envied your relationship with Howard's mother," Amy said. "She's so giving—she never comes to your house without bringing flowers or wine, or little presents for the kids. And whenever she's been on a trip, she always brings you something—remember those lovely Delft bowls she brought you from Amsterdam?"

Now, it was Sara's turn to be amazed. Quietly, she said to Amy, "You know, you're right. I always took those things for granted. I was always so busy focusing on her loud personality that I never took the time to consider the small, thoughtful things she's always done."

Are you, like Sara, closing your eyes to the whole person while zeroing in on one trait or group of behaviors you dislike? Do you take for granted or discount the loving gesture, the unexpected little kindness? The danger inherent here is that you won't recognize the good for cursing the bad—and you'll be the loser all around.

In tangibly acknowledging the niceties and offering credit where it's due, you not only give positive feedback to your in-law, but you also allow *yourself* to acknowledge that she has done something nice. It's a two-step process: first coming to the realization that something positive has happened between you, then manifesting that realization outwardly by showing your appreciation.

The saddest lament I hear from women is this: "I never really appreciated my mother-in-law until she died. There were a million times I could have told her what she meant to me, and I missed every opportunity. Now, it's too late."

It's not too late for you. We tend to spend so much time ruing what we don't have and belittling what we do, that it's wise to take a step back and let the good in the relationship shine through. If you're still looking for the perfect mother-in-law or daughter-in-law after all these years, you're going to be disappointed. Rather, think back on the quiz earlier in this chapter, and focus on the positive aspects of your relationship. You'll both be the better for it.

What are some concrete ways to go about drawing closer? Here are some suggestions:

1. Thank her for small favors. "I appreciate the help with the dishes," you might say to your daughter-in-law. "Thanks for driving little Joey to nursery school," you might say to your mother-in-law. Sounds simple? You'd be amazed at how many people don't bother with these amenities. They just assume they have these things coming to them. Taking a minute to express appreciation builds affection between people.

2. Compliment her in front of others. "Mom makes the best pot roast," you can say when she has friends over for dinner. Or "My daughter-in-law Sue gave a wonderful speech at the Rotary Club last week." As wonderful as it feels to be complimented in private, it's even more gratifying to hear your praises sung in front of others.
3. Write thank-you notes for special gifts and things she's done. Receiving a note written in sincere gratitude makes a person feel cherished and appreciated.
4. Reminisce aloud about past things she's done that you appreciated: "I really liked it when you sent me that recipe for Swedish meatballs that your son loves so much." "Boy, Mom, when you took care of Susannah while I was in the hospital to have Molly, you really took a burden off all of us."
5. Remember her at special times with gifts and cards. Of course, you'll do this on formal occasions such as Mother's Day and her birthday, but how about sending roses to your mother-in-law on *your* wedding anniversary, to show her how much you appreciate the way she raised your husband/her son? Ditto on *his* birthday.

Overall, these in-between years in your marriage can be a time of great peace-making. You're more mature now, you've come through the wrenching uncertainties of early marriage, you've begun to accept your mother-in-law as a real person, not as a cardboard character wearing a sign that says WICKED MOTHER-IN-LAW. You've come to terms with the reality of your relationship: she may never feel good about your working outside the home, but that's okay, too—she appreciates your loving and patient ways with her grandchildren and the support you give her son, your husband.

And you're working hard at trying to negotiate the relationships between the generations, balancing each individual's needs with the others while not totally sacrificing your own. You can do this by being as open and honest as possible, by giving a little and getting a little. It's a skill you began learning as a bride, and have started to polish in the past few years of married life.

If you're the mother-in-law, you've put aside the feeling that this younger woman is going to steal your son away—and come to the delightful conclusion that she hasn't diminished your family, but rather added to it.

Now, together, you can both begin to look down the road to the inevitable time when age and infirmity will begin to take their toll, and you can start thinking of how, together, you can make this next stage as productive and pleasant as possible for everyone involved.

CHAPTER SIX

Special Circumstances

Unlike in fairy tales, not all married people live happily ever after. Neither do all in-law relations. Despite good intentions and honorable efforts, problems sometimes arise that you can neither predict nor prepare for. In this chapter we'll introduce husbands, wives, mothers-in-law, fathers-in-law, and siblings-in-law who have faced some of these "special problems," and offer suggestions and solutions in case you, too, experience similar challenges. First, let's look at problems that arise when couples choose to live together—without a marriage licence.

Heidi fingered the navy-blue bordered invitation in her hand and saw red. There was nothing offensive in the large, cream-colored stationery announcing a sixtieth birthday party for her live-in lover's dad. It was the wording on the envelope that put the fire in her voice as she stormed back into the house after picking up the mail.

"It's addressed to 'Mr. Stan Higham and friend.' And *friend*!"

Heidi raged to Stan, who was reading a novel on the living room sofa. "Your parents know my name as well as I do—why won't they use it? After all, it's not as though we just met last week. We've been living together four years. And I still get an invitation addressed to 'friend.' What do I have to do to get through to your mother and father??"

As common as it is in today's more relaxed atmosphere, living together before—or instead of—marriage can present a battery of problems when it comes to familial relations. Although the parents of live-in lovers are not technically in-laws—the term means related by law—there will still be contact between them and the younger generation. The question, however, is what is the quality of that contact?

In cases like Heidi's and Stan's, where the couple has chosen to commit to each other sans preacher or rabbi, his or her parents may have no objections to the union, but may feel some bewilderment or confusion. If your son is cohabiting with his girlfriend of six years, you may continue to wonder what lies ahead for them. You may be feeling estranged from this young woman who plays such a large role in your son's life. On the continuum that reaches from stranger to friend to family, you may find yourself stuck on the "stranger" end. You may feel trapped in limbo—wishing, perhaps, for some forward motion that shows no signs of appearing.

What you are most likely experiencing is a reluctance to "bond" with this younger woman, for fear—however unjustified—that she just won't be part of your life for very long. In the absence of a permanent symbol of marriage, you are protecting yourself against the time that the relationship between your son and his Heidi unravels. You also may be feeling unbalanced, not clear of your role—are you a mother-in-law? Lover-in-law? Roommate-in-law? The lack of a formal name for what your are adds to the confusion.

The younger woman may be just as unsettled about this tie with an older woman who is family-but-not-family. She may be seeking acceptance, legitimacy, in the eyes of her boyfriend's family. She may complain of being treated like a stranger by the people who mean most to the man she loves most.

When Heidi came to see me about her feelings of distance and her yearning for a closer relationship with Stan's mom, I urged her to be as open with the older woman as possible, not just about her feelings, but also about the couple's plans. My experience is that if the live-in couple lets the parents know the parameters of their relationship from the earliest possible moment, it helps everyone get on more solid footing.

You and your partner should be up-front and candid about your future plans, specifically to allay the kind of tension Heidi was feeling. Again, start with an "I" (or in this case, a "we") statement: "We've decided to live together; we don't have any plans to get married, but we have made a pledge to share our lives this way." Then your partner can reinforce the message by taking his parents aside and assuring them of his commitment to you and urging them to accept you as his mate. "I want you to feel close to Marlena, and hope she will feel close to you," he might say to them.

And for the older generation? Respect your child's decisions, and support the request he has made to accept this woman into your lives as his partner. You also have to recognize the very natural fear you may be experiencing that this relationship is fleeting, and resolve to take a risk. If you don't, you may miss out on being a part of this woman's life while she is a part of your life—which very well could be forever.

Quite different problems arise when your income derives from a family business. What happens when your mother-in-law is not just your husband's mother, but also his . . . boss?

The Family that Works Together

The sign was big and bold, in sweeping red letters on a black background: Jim Smathers and Sons, Auto Parts. There were a chain of them now, up and down the East Coast, and Jim Smathers, who'd built the retail business from the ground up—starting from one small neighborhood body shop—couldn't have been prouder.

For Rusty Smathers, younger son and a manager of the chain's flagship store for the past seven years, it was a different story. Jim Smathers and Sons, Auto Parts, was wreaking havoc on his marriage. His wife, Cindy, told me the story:

"I feel like I have no control over my life. My husband pays more attention to his damn family than he does to me, and his parents are involved in every aspect of my life! I feel as though I have three spouses. This isn't what I bargained for, that's for sure."

Indeed, when Cindy and Rusty met ten years ago, he was a young engineering student full of plans to pursue a graduate degree and land a job with a prestigious corporation. They fell in love, married, and very soon afterward Cindy found herself pregnant. Facing a long haul before he'd be able to support his growing family, Rusty accepted a job offer from his father and had worked for him ever since.

Cindy was never crazy about Jim and his wife, Leslie—she blamed them for keeping Rusty from earning his engineering degree, and she felt now that they played too large a role in her daily life. Cindy was less than thrilled with the salary Rusty was bringing home, but she felt that complaining would upset Rusty's entire family. Not only would she be complaining to her in-laws, she'd also be complaining to her husband's boss and his wife at the same time. Even an offhand comment like, "Gee, I wish we could get away for the weekend" was greeted with a frosty, "Well, the business needs tending to" from her mother-in-law or father-in-law. So she kept her mouth shut—and paid the price in resentment and bitterness.

"It's not only that," Cindy complained. "What's worse is that we have absolutely no privacy. My in-laws know exactly how much my husband makes, they know what hours he works, and they feel they have a right to account for his every hour. If I buy something I love—like a new couch for the den—Leslie's all over me, implying that we can't afford it, that I'm being extravagant. She's probably right, but I hate like hell that she knows it."

Rusty's older brother, Tom, had been in the business for almost fifteen years—and had a fatter paycheck and a cushier office, not to mention the more impressive title of vice president of the company. So in addition to her other resentments, Cindy was coping with a strong dose of jealousy as well.

The situation was, indeed, taking its toll on their marriage. She continually flared up at him for refusing to ask his father for a higher salary and more time off; he responded, predictably, with "Aw, they're my folks. They helped us get on our feet when we needed it. Things are a little tight for them right now—how can I hit them up for more money?"

What Cindy and Rusty were experiencing is very common when father and son (and even mother and daughter) are in business together. The issues that many couples struggle with and master early on in marriage—independence, control over their finances, and the right to make their own decisions—become more complex when in-laws are also the bosses.

What often seems like a dream solution to a young couple's financial woes—hooking up with a thriving family business—can quickly turn into a nightmare.

How can you avoid getting yourself tangled up in a mess like this? Both generations can start by setting some important ground rules, even before your husband or your son reports for his first day of work.

First, both employer and employee (that is, parent and son) must have a very clear idea of the job description and future prospects: How often will I be in line for a raise or a promotion? What are the criteria I will set for my son's advancement? How much vacation will I get after one year? Five years? The tendency is strong, as Cindy and Rusty found, to keep things loose and informal between relatives, but this makes bad business sense. Think, also, of setting up a process whereby the son might report to a neutral third party, rather than to his father. A middle person might lessen the intensity of the business relationship.

Meanwhile, it is also vital to separate business time from pleasure time when the family gets together. You may have to work at this, but keeping the in-law relationship separate from the boss-employee relationship is crucial. For example, you might have to say firmly, "No shop talk tonight" whenever you all get together—and you might have to say it more than once. You may even have to steer the conversation away from bottom lines and spreadsheets over and over. If you establish a pattern, and maybe even ask for help from your sister-in-law (who probably feels the same way you do), the flow of conversation at dinners and social gatherings will become easier, more natural and less business-oriented.

This is a boundary issue, pure and simple. Everyone needs to put distance between personal life and career, and people who work in family businesses are no exception.

Finally, you have to realize that you may be alienating your in-laws if you harbor resentments and bitterness and keep them bottled up. Chances are good that your spouse's parents have no idea how angry you feel. For them, the business is probably a source of joy and pride, not one of hostility and tension. Let them know that you are not blaming them for whatever strains the job is exerting on your marriage; and that you want to be able to talk to them about your hopes and dreams for the future, and that you're afraid they will take your remarks personally. Ditto for complaints. *Tell her*: "If I complain about my husband not being home night after night, I'm complaining to my mother-in-law, not the boss's wife."

Suppose your father-in-law is an ogre of a boss. Your responsibility here is to help your husband separate his professional self from the self who needs approval from Dad—approval that may never be forthcoming. Encourage him to get impartial feedback on his performance from others on the job, point out his accomplishments, and be available to listen to his complaints without criticizing his father. If the situation becomes intolerable, support his decision to work elsewhere.

We've been dealing here with the husband who works for his family's business, but it's just as likely that he could be working for his wife's parents. If this is the case there are certain guidelines everyone can follow to make the situation work. First and foremost, let your husband and your folks handle whatever business problems arise—without your interference. In this situation, your husband is going to be better able to separate boss from parent. Try not to be defensive if your husband comes home with complaints about the job—he's not complaining about your mom or dad, but about his boss. Finally, if it *is* about them as parents, straighten him out. They are *your* parents, they are *his* boss. Keep the issues separate. Realize that your husband's relationship with your parents has to be that of an adult to an adult; they are all mature individuals who can take care of themselves.

Quite another type of problem presents itself when chronic illness strikes someone in the family, as thirty-five-year-old Karen, a journalist with a large daily paper, and her mother-in-law, Alma, learned from bitter firsthand experience.

Coping with Chronic Illness

Karen had an exciting job editing the features section of a metropolitan newspaper, Mitch was chief comedy writer for a popular network sitcom, and they were both crazy in love with Chad, their four-year-old son. Weekends, wife and husband jogged together in the park—she did four miles, he did six—while his mother, Alma, watched Chad; later in the day they'd all get together for a picnic dinner. It doesn't get better than this, Karen and Mitch told each other frequently, with a grin. But it could—and did—get worse.

It began when Karen started dropping things: a reporter's notebook, Chad's Lego blocks, a container of apple juice. At first she laughed it off—"I've got a case of the clumsies," became her running joke—until she also started losing her balance and experiencing episodes of double vision. One day she woke up and couldn't lift her right leg; it felt wooden and dead. In a panic, she visited her doctor and received the horrifying news: At the age of thirty-two, Karen was diagnosed as having multiple sclerosis, a neurological disease whose cure is unknown and whose course is rocky. Its symptoms—including overwhelming fatigue, weakened muscles, visual disturbances, impaired speech—vary in intensity from mild to severe, and it leaves its victims not knowing from day to day what kind of condition they'll be in. It's a devastating illness whose sufferers, like Karen, are often young men and women in their twenties, thirties, and forties.

The diagnosis hit the entire family like a ton of bricks. Normally the most outgoing and energetic of women, Karen withdrew from everyone around her, becoming depressed and apathetic. Mitch grew frantic, not knowing how to cope with an ill wife and an active preschooler who was demanding more and more of his attention. Suprisingly, it was Alma, Karen's mother-in-law, who seemed most devastated. To hear her carry on, one would have thought that *she* had gotten the diagnosis of MS.

At first, she was sympathetic—who wouldn't be? For the first few months after the younger woman got sick, Alma couldn't do enough for her: making dinners, straightening the house, running errands. As time went by and the reality of the disease's permanent nature began to sink in for everyone, Alma started acting strangely. Normally the most helpful, accommodating, and supportive of mothers-in-law, she reacted to Karen's illness brusquely and with little patience. To Karen's requests that Alma watch Chad when Karen was having a bad day, she'd respond with a curt, "Don't pamper yourself so much; the more you do, the stronger you'll feel." She'd shrug off Karen's depression by saying to Mitch, "She's just feeling sorry for herself."

Over and over Alma let her displeasure be known over the fact that Karen couldn't participate in family dinners and other events, that she wasn't "pulling her weight," and that she wasn't functioning as a good mother to Chad.

It was Mitch, totally overwhelmed and in despair, who finally came to see me. Not only was he suddenly the main caretaker for a rambunctious four-year-old, but he was also the referee between two battling women. "I'm caught between the two women I love the most," he said quietly. "Every time my wife and my mother talk to one another, I get a knot in my stomach. And when I try to talk to either one of them, they get mad at *me*!"

When any member of an extended family gets sick, *every* member is affected. When one person suffers, all suffer. That's what was happening in Mitch's family. His mother was upset, disappointed, angry, and scared—feelings very similar to the ones Karen was experiencing. Alma felt bad for her son, who had had an ideal life and now was facing a burden that was only going to get heavier. She grieved for him, and for her grandson—who knew what kind of life *he* was going to face? In her almost inconsolable pain, Alma turned on the person she perceived to be the source of her grief: Karen. Although the rational part of her knew damn well Karen had done nothing to bring this on, in her heart Alma blamed her for wrecking the idyllic life the couple had enjoyed before Karen's devastating illness struck.

Alma's reaction was very typical. The frustration accompanying a chronic illness is devastating. As with any such major upheaval, you will probably find yourself going through a period of mourning. What you've lost is the idealized version of your future, pure and simple. You've lost your faith that tomorrow will be as good as, or better than, today and your ability to look ahead with confidence and good cheer. These are no small losses.

Like Alma, you will have to go through a mourning process, whether you're the primary victim of the disease or one of its secondary victims, such as a spouse, a parent, or an in-law. The famed author Elisabeth Kübler-Ross has outlined the stages in the mourning process, including denial, depression, bargaining, anger, and acceptance. According to Kübler-Ross, a person who is grieving may find herself "stuck" at any one of the stages, and may need help finding her way out.

As Alma found, coming to terms with a crippling illness is never easy. In some families, mutual understanding and communication can make the process a little easier, a little smoother. Other families may need some professional help getting over the rough spots.

If you are involved in a situation like this, it's important to keep the lines of communication open as wide as possible. Information-sharing is crucial; it's the shortages of information that often cause gaps—and gaps create hostility.

In Karen and Alma's case, for example, it would have helped both women to learn as much as possible about multiple sclerosis, and to share their knowledge with each other. If Alma had known, for example, that the disease is characterized by periods of flare-ups and remissions, and that Karen could seem fine one day and be totally incapacitated the next, she probably would have better understood her daughter-in-law's limitations—and her depression.

If you're in Alma's shoes, find out everything you can about your relative's condition. Read up on it in magazines, newspapers and books, or ask to go with her to the doctor if she doesn't mind, so that you can hear firsthand about what she's experiencing.

The more you know about the course of the illness—whether it's multiple sclerosis, cancer, heart disease, kidney failure, or any other major condition—the better you will be able to help your loved ones plan for the future. You will be able to decide what you can and cannot give them, in terms of financial support, childcare, and emotional input. A family meeting, with all parties sharing their needs and their expectations, can go a long way toward easing this weight on all of you.

If your husband is in Mitch's situation, and much of the burden is falling on him to referee between you and your mother-in-law, you have to help him find a way to extricate himself from that uncomfortable middle ground. Now is the time for him to be totally honest with his mother, letting her know how upset Mitch is, that he won't tolerate her treating you poorly. Clearly, no one *chooses* to be struck by a devastating illness, and innuendos that you're not "trying hard enough" or that you did something to "bring this on yourself" just add to the overall misery everyone is feeling.

He also needs to let his mother know that he needs support for himself, and the reassurance that he can come to her and talk about his concerns and worries without fearing that she will point the finger of blame at you. *And* he needs to know that she'll be there for your children, when and if the time comes that you both need her.

As unwelcome a guest as illness is in a household, it has the potential to bring together family members, who often unite to battle the unwanted condition together. Nicole, on the other hand, a twenty-five-year-old pharmacist, faced a completely different situation, one that easily could have driven a wedge between father and son.

"My Father-in-law Is Coming On to Me"

The very first night they met, Keith told Nicole all about his father, Stan. Hunched over coffee (hers) and hot chocolate (his) in the college student center, they talked about their respective families, and Keith confided to this new young woman he'd just met that he'd always had mixed feelings about Stan, with his easy charm, his debonair good looks, and his social graces. Reticent Keith admitted that he admired his dad, but that he felt a certain envy, as well.

Later, when Nicole was introduced to the man who would become her father-in-law, she secretly felt that Keith was exaggerating. Indeed, she found Stan personable, warm, and charming, and she was impressed by his social know-how. Nicole could not understand why Keith wanted to keep his distance from his father, who lived alone, having been divorced for many years. She sensed a certain push/pull in the relationship Keith had with Stan; her husband was both fascinated and repelled by the man he called "Pop."

When Nicole and Keith had been married three years, Keith found the competition less and less to his liking, and he began turning down more and more of Stan's invitations. As he met with one rejection after another from his son, Stan began to circumvent Keith and go directly to Nicole. On the phone, he would complain about his son, in a way that made Nicole uncomfortable. "Keith doesn't know how to show you a good time. You're a young and attractive woman, you need someone who will take you places and show you off," Stan would say.

Troubled by his comments, and not quite sure how to respond, Nicole simply changed the subject. Stan's little digs about Keith, however, left her feeling vaguely dismayed and unsettled. She couldn't put her finger on the exact cause; she just knew things weren't quite as they should be. Then Stan invited her to lunch.

Her father-in-law chose an intimate French restaurant, and greeted Nicole with a bouquet of pink roses. He ordered wine and appetizers for them both. Over the coq-au-vin, Stan put his arm around her, held her hand, and began questioning Nicole about her feelings for her husband. He also began repeating his earlier suggestion—"Maybe Keith's not the right man for you."

Suddenly, Nicole was feeling *very* uncomfortable. Although she admitted later that she'd been pretty naive until that point, she suddenly got the very clear message that Stan was looking to take his son's place! She now had an excellent idea of his intentions—and they weren't honorable.

"I didn't have the foggiest idea what to do: whether to slap his face and walk out, or whether to pretend nothing was happening," Nicole told me later. "This was Keith's *father*, for God's sake. I didn't want to offend him, but I didn't want to just sit there and let him think I was available. And then I had the crazy thought: What if I'm *wrong*? What if I'm imagining the whole thing?"

Clearly, she wasn't imagining it, and clearly she had to do *something*. In a daze Nicole excused herself from the table, made up a story about how her boss was expecting her back at the drugstore, she had a prescription to fill, customers were waiting . . . and ran out of the restaurant.

Back at work with some time and space to clear her head,

Nicole found a new dilemma facing her. Should she tell Keith about the episode, or let the whole thing drop? If she told her husband about what happened, she ran the risk of destroying the already tenuous relationship between the two men. If she kept quiet, she ran the equally unsavory risk of having her father-in-law come on to her again. And again.

It was a no-win situation. Even more worrisome was this tiny little doubt nagging away at the very back of her mind: What if she, Nicole, had done something to encourage Stan? Did she bring this on herself?

The sort of problem Nicole was facing is, unfortunately, not all that uncommon. It happens more frequently than most people realize. Lots of in-laws fantasize about each other; that's pretty normal when families are thrown together. Your brother-in-law may get a little flirtatious, your father may think your sister-in-law is a hot little number. When fantasy gives way to reality, though, the relative has clearly overstepped his boundaries.

In some ways a pass made by an overeager father-in-law can be seen as an abuse of power. As the older, more settled, and presumably more mature individual in the relationship, he should have the restraint and the self-control to keep his libido in check.

If he doesn't—what can you do? You, like Nicole, may think you have two alternatives here—neither of them particularly pleasant. You could talk to your husband about the incident, running the risk that the knowledge that his father came on to you will so enrage him that it will spark an angry confrontation between father and son. Or you could ignore your father-in-law's advances, hoping that you were imagining things or, if you weren't, that he won't do it again. This path is risky, at best, since it's a given that you will have social contact with this man over and over in the future. It's also now a given that you will be uncomfortable in his presence, and that your unease will add tension to all future family gatherings.

Actually, there is a third option, and that is to go directly to your father-in-law and confront him outright with your dismay. "I was very upset about our conversation over lunch, Dad. I felt angry that you were coming on to me, and *I did not like it.* Do not do that again." He may deny anything happened ("Aw, honey, I was just being friendly"), or he may throw the blame back on you ("But you sat there looking so pretty in that sexy dress. . . ."). Don't allow it. Your father-in-law *did* act inappropriately, and you have to be prepared to act to stop it from happening again. *Tell him so.* "If you ever, ever do that again, I will go right to Keith." And you have to be ready to carry through on your threat.

This is an instance where you have every right to put your foot down. Realize that the fault is not yours, but the responsibility to stop this from going any further is. When you encounter behavior like this it's easy to question your own role in it: Did I do something to bring this on? Was I suggestive in my language? Was my skirt too short, my blouse too low-cut? You may also begin to question your own grasp on reality: *Was* I making the whole thing up in my mind? Was this my overheated imagination at play?

Listen to that inner voice that says you weren't fantasizing. Trust that voice, go with it. And don't carry around the secret deep inside you, as though *you* are the one at fault.

Clearly, you have to confront your father-in-law, because, one hopes, you are going to be in a relationship with his son for a good long time. Avoiding contact with this older man will be difficult and awkward at best. You have the right—yes, the right—to threaten to reveal all to his son. And he has to know that you will carry through.

We've discussed that it is not at all unusual for one in-law to be attracted to another. What happens when that attraction is reciprocal? Beverly, a slightly chunky thirty-eight-year-old woman whose thick, curly brown hair had a wide streak of gray, faced that very situation within her own family.

An Affair That's All in the Family

She probably could have seen the signs months earlier, but she chose to ignore them. Beverly and Jay, a stockbroker, had been married eleven years and had four children: eight years old, six, four, and two. Bev's younger sister, Samantha, loved playing aunt. She was single, with a demanding job as a toy buyer for a large department store, and she would bring the kids samples of new games and stuffed animals to try out before they hit the shelves. On occasion, Samantha would volunteer to baby-sit; Jay would work late, and Beverly would run errands. All too frequently, Jay arrived home first, and Beverly, coming in the door an hour or so later, would hear adult laughter coming from the family room. Samantha and Jay would be hunched over a board game, heads together, while the children slept upstairs in the bedrooms.

"I should have opened my eyes, but the thought of my little sister and my husband being attracted to each other just seemed too . . . unbelievable. I mean, that sort of thing doesn't happen," Bev said to me in an emergency session.

Why the emergency? Because the previous evening, Beverly had returned home from the library to find Jay and Samantha together again, but this time in the master bedroom. Totally unclothed.

Now, as she sat sobbing in my office, Beverly wondered how

she could ever again trust two people whom she loved deeply—and who, she felt bitterly, had turned that love against her.

"It feels as though I've been hit by a truck—no, *two* trucks. I've been doubly betrayed," she cried, discarding tissue after damp tissue. After a horrendous scene the night before, which left all three participants thoroughly drained and shaken, Beverly had learned that Jay and her sister had been having an affair for the past six months. "God, I still can't believe it. My husband and my sister! It feels almost like . . . incest."

Indeed, I could sympathize with Beverly. Any affair involving the extended family has the incest taboo attached to it, especially when in-laws have been close. What this young woman had to realize was that as distasteful and sordid as the whole episode felt, it really was not technically incest because no blood relatives were directly involved.

That doesn't make the situation any less difficult to deal with, of course. When in-laws become involved sexually, the regular family roles blur, family gatherings become tense and strained, and family unity is stretched—possibly to the breaking point. It is tragic enough if your husband is having an affair with a stranger; if he is making love to your cousin, there is an added element of betrayal that makes it harder to forgive and forget.

If you are facing this kind of situation, my urgent advice is to seek professional help. You need someone to help you sort through the miasma of emotions you are feeling now—anger, bewilderment, betrayal, uncertainty about the future. You need someone to help you evaluate the status of *both* relationships that have been threatened—that with your spouse, and that with your sibling (or with whichever relative is involved). Finally, you need someone to help you develop a plan for the future.

Don't automatically assume that your marriage is over if you've discovered an infidelity. Many married people have an unwritten and maybe even unspoken contract with themselves: If I ever find out that my spouse is having an affair, I will end the marriage immediately. Often, this is a vow taken fairly early in wedded life, before the idea of an affair is anything more than a nebulous *thing* that happens to other people. Now that it's a reality, don't feel locked into keeping that vow. At this point, it's essential to look at all the circumstances. Many, many marriage counselors and family therapists advise that it is not impossible to forgive an infidelity. Only *you* can decide what's best for you. When you're making that decision, don't be swayed by a belief system you created years ago.

If you've decided to keep the marriage intact, one guideline that is almost inviolable is *not to share the intimate details with other family members*. I would caution this with any affair, but it becomes more crucial when an in-law is involved. If the rest of the family knows what has gone on between your husband and your sister, for example—how many times they met at the Golden Flamingo Hotel, how many times they found occasion to steal away together for a weekend in Cape Cod—it makes it doubly hard for you and your spouse to put the incident behind you and move on. Once this becomes part of family lore, you will always feel that someone is talking about you. Since these are people with whom you will be thrown together over and over, remember that discretion is the better part of valor.

You may be faced with a moral dilemma of an entirely different sort if the affair is being carried out by an in-law with someone else—and you stumble upon it inadvertently. What do you do if you, like Loretta, suspect that your sister-in-law is cheating on her husband?

Loretta, a bookkeeper who had been married to Tony for eight years, was out to lunch with a friend when she caught a glimpse of Tony's sister, Eve, at a nearby table. Loretta didn't know the handsome man Eve was sitting with, but there were two things she did know: He was not Eve's husband, and the two did not look as though they wanted to be disturbed. For Loretta, the encounter validated a long-held suspicion that her sister-in-law was involved in an extramarital affair. Eve had been dodging Loretta's invitations to get together by pleading that she had no time. Loretta had also noticed that her husband's sister had been taking special pains with her appearance lately—she'd got a new sexy haircut and started wearing slightly tighter clothes and slightly higher heels.

Now, Loretta was faced with the challenge of what to do with this unwelcome and unsolicited information. Approach Eve with it later? Dump it on her husband? Call a family meeting and trumpet the news to all the world?

Certainly not the latter. First, I would tell Loretta, try to establish quietly and discreetly how much anyone else knows. If, at the next family gathering, there's talk about Eve, don't volunteer any information until you can ascertain how much the others know. Let them set the pace for the discussion. If, for example, your mother-in-law asks if you've noticed anything different about Eve, you could respond, "What do *you* think is up?" rather than blurting out that you saw her at a restaurant holding hands with a stranger. Spreading rumors about your sister-in-law's supposed infidelity can only get you into trouble.

With your husband, you have to phrase the information in a way that is honest and not accusatory. "I bumped into your sister at La Circe the other day, and she was with some guy I never saw before" is a more tactful and honest statement than "I saw your sister with another man, and I think they are having an affair." This allows you to tell him what you saw rather than speculating about what you *think* might have been going on.

Finally, do you confront your sister-in-law head-on with what you think you know? No—what's the purpose? Respect her privacy as you would that of a friend. I'm not suggesting that you lie, but neither am I suggesting that you run as fast as you can to inform her of your assumption.

Even as extramarital affairs involving in-laws can put a severe strain on a relationship, the realities of dysfunctional families can lead to stresses both within a marriage and within an extended family unit. Having a family member who is drug- or alcohol-dependent, or one who is the victim of a long-term mental or emotional illness, poses a challenge that calls for patience, flexibility, and maturity, as my clients Tracey and Stuart learned—painfully.

An In-law Under the Influence

Stuart, a quiet blond bear of a man in his late thirties, couldn't remember a time when his mother, Roberta, didn't drink. She ruined his fifth birthday party by screaming at all the children, then passing out on the dining-room table; she could barely walk a straight line at his junior-high graduation, and she never made it to his high school graduation at all—she was sleeping it off on the living-room sofa. The young graduate was both bitterly disappointed that his mother was not at the graduation, and relieved that there'd be no scene in the football stadium when he accepted his diploma.

When Stuart was courting Tracey, he made no secret of the fact that Roberta drank, but only as she got deeper and deeper into the relationship did Tracey, a computer programmer with an interest in nature, begin to hear the real horror stories. As Roberta's blackouts escalated, so did Tracey's discomfort, but her love for Stuart overcame her misgivings, and the couple was married. Roberta managed to stay sober for the ceremony, and for most of the reception following.

Within four years Tracey had two young children, and ever-graver concerns. Her mother-in-law kept insisting on seeing her grandchildren—Brooke, three, and Courtney, one—and Tracey lived in fear that the little girls would be terrified if they saw the older woman drunk. She'd seen Roberta lash out at Stuart and his father, Herb, when she'd had her customary one too many, and Tracey was determined that her children would not be subject to the same verbal abuse.

And things were getting worse with Stuart.

"He and I are fighting all the time now," Tracey said. "His mother calls, and he runs. She disappoints him and hurts him over and over again, and he just takes it. I want him to break off his relation with her until she dries out, but he refuses."

"She's my mother," Stuart replied quietly but with determination. "I can't just desert her. She's my mother."

One individual's dysfunction or illness disrupts the structure and the rhythm of an entire family. The lines of authority are broken, and often there is role reversal or exchange: The child may become the "parent" of a drug-dependent mother; a son may become the "husband" when his father is emotionally paralyzed with chronic depression. All family relationships are thrown into turmoil—including those between in-laws. There is quite often a contagious sense of depression and anxiety in families like this. One of your challenges will be to avoid "catching" the overall mood of tension and succumbing to the depression.

In Tracey's case, where her mother-in-law was an alcoholic, many factors were at play. Tracey was worried, privately, that her husband would become an alcoholic like his mother. She resented Roberta because of the pain Roberta had inflicted on Stuart, and continued to inflict now on his family. She felt gypped out of a normal relationship with her mother-in-law. It's almost impossible to create ties with a woman who is alternately loud and abusive and then weepy and ultimately unconscious. Finally, she was angry at the rest of the family for their seeming acceptance of Roberta's drinking.

Whether the problem is alcoholism, as in Roberta's case, or any other substance abuse, or whether there has been a history of mental illness, you, as the in-law—often still perceived as the "newcomer" or the "outsider" in the family—may be the least able to tolerate the situation. In frustration and dismay you may eventually point out that it *isn't* normal for mothers to pass out at Fourth of July barbecues or for fathers to be so zonked out on tranquilizers that they don't recognize their own grandchildren.

Chances are good that your observations will not be warmly received. Other family members, having built up layer upon layer of insulation against the situation, may deny outright that a problem exists. A lot of adult children of alcoholics, for example, simply do not realize that theirs is not a normal family; they genuinely may not have identified the fact that a problem exists. In cases of mental illness family members may be so used to a bizarre behavior—a mother who is so depressed she doesn't speak for weeks, for example, or a brother who won't leave the house unaccompanied—that they have become desensitized to its existence. They may resent what they see as your meddling.

You, as the newcomer, are going to have to proceed cautiously. There may be the natural tendency to ignore as everyone else is ignoring the unpleasant situation. Unfortunately, the behavior will continue to dominate the family, whether it's acknowledged or not. Your best bet may be to tackle things head-on by asking questions.

"It seems to me," you might say, "that most of the time we're together, your mother seems to be drinking a lot, that she's not in control. Do you think she's an alcoholic?" Your spouse and the other family members might deny at first that a problem exists, but my experience shows that, ultimately, they will probably be relieved to have the truth out in the open.

If the denial continues, and you really believe there is a problem, you need to get some professional help to deal with it on a day-to-day basis, find new ways to confront the issue, and come to grips with the reality of the situation.

Bringing other people in—with discretion, of course—is another useful strategy, especially if your spouse and you don't agree on the severity of the problem. If you feel pretty certain that your mother-in-law is suffering from a mental illness, but your husband doesn't agree, try talking your concerns out with your clergyperson or, even better, your family doctor. You will want to know and *need* to know if your mother-in-law's symptoms can be passed down from generation to generation; will your husband be subject to the same "spells"? Your children? These are questions you can rightly take to a doctor.

What if you have a genuine concern about the safety of your children if they are left with an impaired grandparent, and your spouse refuses to agree that anything is seriously wrong? Your first and foremost priority is the safety of those children. When you confront your husband with your reasons for not allowing Kim or Brad to stay alone with his father, have a concrete list ready as your "evidence": "Last week, when I went to pick up the kids at his house, your father was fast asleep on the couch with a cigarette in his hand." "Your mother was weaving all over the road when she took Kimmie home from ballet yesterday."

Solicit help from other family members if you need it. My friend Judy, alarmed by what she saw as her mother-in-law's increasing dependence on the bottle and her decreasing ability to function, sought out her sister-in-law, Amelia. The two women discussed the problem and went *together* to their husbands, armed with concrete evidence of their mother's problem. Working in tandem, they convinced the two men that a hazardous condition existed. Then, together, all four convinced the older woman to start attending Alcoholics Anonymous meetings at a local church.

You might also look into a technique called "confrontational intervention," which is frequently used to break down the denial that is so common to someone with a drug or alcohol problem. Using this method, a whole family gathers together and gently confronts the one who has the problem in an atmosphere of caring and warmth. There are no accusations, no insults, just a stating of the situation and many, many offers of support.

In general, there are several rules and guidelines you can follow if you find yourself part of a family in which one member has a serious problem:

1. Be compassionate and understanding. Often, in your anger, dismay and concern about yourself and your immediate family, you might lose sight of the fact that your in-law is truly suffering. Acknowledging this goes a long way toward easing hard feelings between you.
2. Keep in mind that people can change. Don't give up on your alcoholic sister-in-law because you think she's a hopeless case. Many "hopeless cases" are now fully functioning recovering alcoholics. If she *does* give up the bottle, don't hold her past behavior against her. That would undermine her achievement and continue to put obstacles in the path toward any sound relationship you might build together.
3. Be patient and flexible. Your brother-in-law might not recover as quickly as *you* would like; there may be setbacks. Don't come down too hard on him for backsliding. Be supportive. If he needs to attend an Alcoholics Anonymous meeting the night of a holiday dinner, push the dinner back to accommodate him—it'll be worth it in the long run.
4. Bring issues out into the open. Keeping secrets leads to increased emotional stress, both on the part of the alcoholic

and the drug abuser, and on the part of the in-law. Keeping things hidden allows problems to seep down to the next generation . . . and the next.

5. Know when to seek professional help, both for the one who has the problem and for the rest of the family. Resources can include a mental-health professional, a physician, a clergyperson, a drug-rehabilitation counselor, or anyone who has the training with your particular problem. You don't have to go it alone.
6. Know when to alert the authorities. Suicidal behavior, drunken driving, frequent disappearances—these are cases where you need to turn to the police for their intervention. Be fully aware of the consequences here: If you do call the police because your drunken mother-in-law is about to step into a car, you are apt to bring the wrath of your in-law's family down on you. If you *don't*, can you live with the consequences if your mother-in-law's car, out of control, strikes and cripples a child? Your first line of defense, of course, is your husband and his siblings; but if they won't act, you may have to take control. The rest of the family may be angry at first, but I predict they will fall into line.

Sexual Abuse

Incurring the wrath of the entire family is also a risk when you're dealing with another dysfunction: sexual abuse. Nina learned that to her horror when she confronted her husband with the information that his brother, Gus, had been abusing the couple's elder daughter.

Nina and Ralph, married twelve years, treasured the relationship their daughters, Valerie, nine, and Lindsay, five, shared with their uncle Gus. Lately, though, Val had become very quiet and withdrawn when Gus was scheduled to visit, and had to be encouraged to go to the zoo or the playground with him. The once-cheerful and outgoing child had also begun to have tantrums, and her fourth-grade teacher had mentioned to Nina that her attention span had decreased.

Everything suddenly became horribly clear to Nina one night while she was helping Valerie get ready for her bath, and the child began to sob, "Mommy, I don't want to be with Uncle Gus anymore. Do I have to?" With some gentle questioning, Nina encouraged Valerie to share what was troubling her. "Uncle Gus touches me on the privates, and he tells me not to tell anyone. He said if I told, you and Daddy would be angry at me—and that you would say I'm a liar."

The problem of child sexual abuse is common—more common than you or I would like to believe. Moreover, an estimated 80 to 90 percent of all children who are sexually abused are, like Valerie, victims of someone they love and trust. Indeed, in half the cases, the abuser is the father or the stepfather.

Neither, sadly, is it uncommon for a child to be abused by a beloved uncle. The violation of trust is all the more damaging than if the abuser had been a clerk in the local supermarket or a camp counselor. There is also the element of disbelief that enters into it: How could *my* brother be a pervert? Not Gus!

This is the reaction Nina got when she took her troubling news to her husband. Ralph refused to entertain the notion that his younger brother might have acted improperly toward his daughter. Shocked and bewildered, but firmly convinced that Valerie had not made up the story, Nina took the little girl immediately to her pediatrician, both to ascertain that no physical damage had been done and to enlist an ally in her lonely battle.

In cases like Valerie's, it is of utmost importance to support the child, and to reassure her that you believe her story and that you are doing everything you can to end the abuse. Because doctors are required by law to report suspected cases of abuse, and because the court system is usually prompt to step in, Nina got a restraining order forbidding Gus to come near her daughter. Her "victory" came at a price—the rest of the family, angered that Nina had "washed the family linen in public," hurled bitter words at her. Even Ralph, her husband, felt she had overreacted and had overstepped her bounds.

Had she? No. Nina's first and most urgent obligation was to her child. The most important message you can give to a youngster who has been abused is that you believe her and that you are willing to deal with the consequences of the family's disapproval rather than deny the abuse. Tragically, it happens all too often that a family plays into the psychology of abuse, needing desperately to believe that it doesn't really exist—and certainly not in their family.

Suppose you are in this type of situation and all your in-laws (not to mention your husband) are aligned against you? Your mother-in-law is angry because you brought dishonor upon her son; your husband is disgusted because he thinks you believe your daughter more than you care for him and because his brother has been disgraced in the community. It's an extreme case, of course, but it happens. Support from the professional community—doctors, mental-health workers, therapists—is more crucial now, perhaps, than at any other time. You cannot do this alone. Your friends, your child's teachers, your own parents—all of these are possible allies during this painful and frightening time.

The key here is also realizing that you did what you had to in order to prevent further psychological damage to your child. You may have risked your marriage, and you will have to deal with that. But you have protected your daughter from a nightmare that could haunt her well into her adult years.

Nina's case *was* extreme. The breakdown of the marriage is not inevitable in cases of in-law sexual abuse. In many instances, as evidence comes out to support a child's story—whether through a doctor's examination or in court testimony, or even through the admission of the abuser—family members will rally around the child, and their overwhelming desire to keep her from further pain will win out over their desire to protect the abuser.

Yes, you are likely to meet with some denial at first if you come to the family with accusations of child molestation. In all too many cases, an offender will have been a victim of abuse himself—this is a pattern that tends to repeat itself, being handed down from generation to generation with no one acknowledging its presence. Part of the psychology of abuse is that the more it's covered up, the more it can flourish. If you learn, to your horror, that your husband's father, his brother, or his cousin has been fondling your child, you can safely assume that that person himself has known abuse as a child. You can also make sure that he is never left alone with your child again—and that you keep a vigilant eye out on how he interacts with other children.

Summing Up

As much as we'd all love it, we don't live in a fairy-tale world. Storybook marriages do exist, but so do chemically dependent fathers-in-law, alcoholic mothers-in-law, seriously mentally ill sisters-in-law. Fathers-in-law make passes at their sons' wives. Young brides or grooms are diagnosed with crippling illnesses. Family businesses demand a husband's total fealty. Uncles abuse young nieces or nephews.

In all families, communication is important, but in families in which these unusual circumstances exist, communication is *vital*. Families in which the normal ties have broken down, in which tension and stress are as much a part of the daily diet as peanut-butter sandwiches—these are the families that demand an increased level of openness and honesty. Tolerance and compassion are the order of the day.

The key to all of the unusual circumstances we've talked about here is creative problem-solving. Use other people as resources as often as possible; you don't have to reinvent the wheel. Be open to partial solutions: You may not succeed in getting your mother-in-law to put down the bottle, but you can come to an understanding with your husband that your children will never be passengers in a car she is driving. You may not have been able to prevent your husband from sleeping with your sister, but you can arrive at mutual forgiveness and newfound closeness if he ends the affair. Your daughter-in-law might not recover from her debilitating illness, but you can help her build a life that is full and rewarding anyway.

Be flexible. Accept trade-offs or compromises for the sake of family peace and unity. Don't be afraid that you will hurt your in-law's feelings if you speak out honestly and confront situations directly. Keeping your fears and tensions hidden can only result in a buildup of resentment, which in turn results in withdrawal, either physical or emotional. A few hurt feelings are easier to mend than a relationship that has been allowed to deteriorate completely.

CHAPTER SEVEN
AGING TOGETHER

Terri, a stocky brunette of thirty-nine with a tired smile, and Greg, a high school chemistry teacher, had been married nine years when her father died. Terri's mother, Jeannette, left a widow with no means of supporting herself, moved in with the couple and their daughter, Samantha. Greg couldn't have been more understanding and supportive when his mother-in-law came to stay; he fixed up a second-floor bedroom for her and made her feel welcome.

Because Jeannette didn't drive, Terri ferried her everywhere: to the supermarket, to the beauty parlor, to the doctor's office. With all the time she spent with her own mother, Terri had very little time for Greg's seventy-one-year-old mom, Hilda. Terri didn't particularly care for her mother-in-law, and Greg never pushed her to invite Hilda for dinner or to initiate any social gathering.

Then Hilda, like Jeannette a widow, had a heart attack.

Greg had a married brother, but as the oldest son he felt a

strong responsibility to Hilda. When she was released after a week in the hospital's coronary-care unit, it was to Greg and Terri's house that she came to recuperate. The couple rented a hospital bed and set it up in the first-floor den, and tried to settle into the new routine. It was just for a short time, they assured each other, until Hilda got back on her feet.

It wasn't easy. Suddenly, Terri was responsible for caring for two elderly women and an eleven-year-old daughter, who rightfully wanted her mother to be available to help chaperone school trips, attend piano recitals, and lead the local Girl Scout troop. Terri's mother expected to be driven to the pharmacy when her arthritis medicine ran out, her mother-in-law needed to be escorted to the bathroom at hourly intervals, and her husband expected her to be warm, loving—oh, yes, and sexy—after he'd had a hard day with seventy-five 11th-graders and a demanding principal.

"God, it can't get any worse," Terri told herself. She was wrong.

Hilda fell and broke her hip on the way back from the bathroom. Now, she was totally immobilized, and needed twenty-four-hour-a-day attention; she had to be brought her meals in bed and helped on and off a bedpan. Terri very quickly, very desperately, thought she would go completely out of her mind.

It's not usually this dramatic, but the process of aging is inevitable, and it affects not only the elderly, but also everyone around them. What Terri was going through—although extreme—mirrors the experience of many families as they navigate their way through the rocky terrain of aging.

America is graying. People are living longer, so it is more likely than not that you will have the responsibility at one point in your marriage of taking care of an elderly parent or in-law; if not actually tending to them in your home, at least making decisions about their medical needs and living arrangements.

We'll talk about the caretaking role—and why women are more likely than men to be cast into it. We'll talk about the conflict this creates in a marriage and the tensions that can arise between husband and wife when they are dealing with elderly, frail, and needy parents. We'll look at ways you can make the responsibilities a little less burdensome, and offer some guidelines for lightening the load. Finally, we'll explore concrete ways to resolve such difficult issues as making alternative living arrangements for your ailing in-laws, discussing your in-laws' wishes for wills and funeral arrangements, and helping your elderly in-laws maintain their dignity in the face of increasing frailty and debilitation.

Because aging is a lifelong process, there is often no one episode you can point to and say, "Aha, *that's* when my father-in-law started getting old." He may complain a bit more about aches and pains, or he may forget your son's birthday or your anniversary. Life-cycle events can highlight or accelerate the process—your father-in-law's retirement after an active career, for example, may make you realize suddenly that he's no longer the vital, vibrant rock you always thought he was. The death of a spouse can often leave the remaining parent more fragile, more vulnerable—and can accelerate the ravages of aging.

Dealing with the death of an in-law—and with the physical and emotional needs of the surviving spouse—is a challenge you are likely to face at some point in your married life. In one respect, a daughter-in-law can function on a more objective level when an in-law is dying. While your husband is dealing with his overwhelming grief, you can provide support and care for him and for his surviving parent. Although you may have dearly loved your father-in-law, in reality, his death is somewhat less a blow for you than for your husband and, obviously, than for your mother-in-law. So your job is to encourage the members of the family to consult each other in terms of making large decisions—

those concerning life-support systems, for example, or funeral arrangements—while tactfully staying out of those arrangements yourself.

You also have to accept the fact that this may be a time when your husband is much more involved with his family of origin than with his family of choice. He may be at the hospital day and night while his father battles cancer; he may be on the telephone six or seven times a day with brothers and sisters in the days immediately following the funeral. Don't be threatened by this; it's natural. Understand that his mother desperately needs her children around her at this time of bereavement, and encourage your husband to be available to her as much as she needs him. This is not a time to put your needs first.

A New Role

As a bride, then a wife and mother, you probably rarely if ever thought you were going to be responsible for your aging parents or your spouse's parents. Suddenly, you're being called upon more and more to adopt this new role. You drive your mother-in-law to the pharmacy; take your father-in-law for his annual checkup with the ophthalmologist, then chauffeur him to get his new prescription for glasses filled. This is probably all happening at a time when you have adolescent or teenage children making demands on you. You may also have a full-time job that drains much of your time, attention, and energy.

How did you find yourself in this mess? Despite the monumental societal changes over the past several decades, the role of caretaker still falls overwhelmingly on the woman. As much as women are represented in the work force in numbers approaching those of men, women are still what sociologist Lucy Rose Fischer calls the "kinkeepers." According to this professor at the University of Minnesota, women tend to the chores that keep families together: buying and mailing the birthday and anniversary cards, planning the Thanksgiving dinners, presiding over the family calendars. For many women who have been the cornerstone of their extended families since the day they said "I do," seguing from this role into the role of caretaker is only natural.

In times of crisis—illness, aging—it's the women more often than the men who accept the burden. Some women don't even see it as a burden; some do it willingly because it fulfills their need to feel important and central to the family's well-being. Others may view this caretaking as a way of "repaying" a debt for care they received in the past.

Who is most likely to find herself shouldering this type of responsibility? Studies have shown that *you* are if:

1. Your mother-in-law has no daughters.
2. You are married to the oldest son in the family.
3. You live geographically closest to your in-laws.
4. You never learned to say no.

Wittingly or unwittingly, husbands often encourage women to take on the chores of caring for their parents by ceding over the role of adult children to their wives. "Will you take my mother to the allergist tomorrow afternoon?" comes the innocent request. "I have to be in court then." "Will you call the Medicare office and see what happened to Dad's check? You're better at dealing with these kinds of things over the phone." "Will you pick up a few things for Mother next time you're out shopping?"

Little by little, you find you're doing more and more and liking it less. You're stretched thinner than onionskin, you're resenting your husband's lack of participation, and you're feeling bitter toward your mother-in-law—whom you may not have felt particularly close to even *before* she became so dependent on you.

It helps, at this point, to understand *why* you're feeling so used and abused. Why is parenting a parent or a parent-in-law so difficult? One reason is that caring for an elderly person takes very different skills—and fosters different emotions—than taking care of a young child. You were probably tolerant of your daughter's mistakes or limitations when she was a toddler. If she had an accident and wet her pants, you expected that—and you comforted and reassured her as you changed her wet panties. When your father-in-law is incontinent, there's no comfort and acceptance; you are much more likely to feel embarrassed and annoyed. He should know better, you think to yourself. Damned if I'm going to wash his soiled underclothes.

So, in addition to the very real demands on your time and energy, there is the psychological component of resentment. You have to walk a very careful line between caring for others and caring for yourself. The struggle for many women is that they get a lot of positive feedback for taking on the role of caretaker, but they are also bombarded with the message that they must also take care of themselves and feel self-fulfilled. "What a joke," they mutter bitterly. "I can hardly find time to brush my teeth at night, and this magazine article is telling me I should go to the gym three times a week to work out. Hah!"

After one of my in-law workshops—this one in Michigan—I received a heartfelt letter from a woman who had heard me speak about the challenges of the so-called "Sandwich Generation"—those caught between children and elderly parents.

"Dear Penny,

"You could have been talking directly to me in your session at the church. When I'm taking care of my mother-in-law, who is in bed after a stroke, I feel guilty that I'm not home for my teenage children; when I'm with my children, I worry about how my mother-in-law is doing. Then one day it struck me: There's really no time for *me*. I don't have the time to do the things I need to do—exercise, go to the beauty parlor, shop for clothes—let alone the things I would like to do, such as just sitting on the porch one morning and reading a book. I'm wondering how I can fix it so there's some time for myself."

This woman is far from alone. As parents age, women feel themselves pulled in so many different directions. In a humorous little feature called "The working woman's lament: WHAT sex life?!" [*Redbook*, March 1989] Sylvia Hughes, a Canadian comedy writer, presents a list of "Things to Do Today." They include:

1. Finish annual report for boss
2. Pick up kids
3. Go shopping
4. Take dog to vet
5. Fix dinner
6. Call mother-in-law
7. Do laundry
8. Have sex (optional)

The list is part of a bittersweet and funny essay—"We used to have lifestyle. We used to have a sex life. Now we just have a family," the wife observes to the husband—but it illustrates remarkably well the bind you are likely to find yourself in at this point in your marriage. Luckily, there are some steps you can take to ease the burden and make life a little easier. If you are feeling the pull of multiple generations, try some of these techniques:

1. Identify the Problem. Start by making a list of everybody's needs—including your own. Then put the items in order of priority. Take the last third of the list and throw it away. Yes, throw it away. If they're really important, those items you've discarded will wind up back on the list sooner or later. In the meantime, you've given yourself some mental breathing space.
2. Find time during the day to do something for yourself. When you make your list of things you have to do, work into it half

an hour to sit and read the newspaper, an hour to work in the rose garden (if this is something you love, not another burden), forty-five minutes to soak in a bubble bath. Make sure that when you chop off the bottom third of that list, *your* needs aren't among the victims. Also, don't feel that you have to get everything on your list done before you turn to your own needs. Taking a few minutes in the middle of the day can help you recharge your batteries to better attack the rest of the agenda.

3. Learn to say no. Remember the techniques you learned in Chapter 3. Now's the time to brush up on them again: Practice role-playing with a friend. Imagine the worst-possible-case scenario if you said no. It's tempting to try to be all things to all people, but you run the risk of running yourself into the ground by doing this.
4. Seek out help. This is essential; you simply cannot do everything yourself. Have someone share the burden. If high on your list of priorities is grocery shopping for your homebound father-in-law in the next town, try to find a high school kid living nearby who would love to earn a few dollars and have him or her do the shopping. Many religious organizations have agencies that provide services for the elderly; see if a facility such as a nearby Jewish Family Service or the Catholic Charities in your community can send someone to your mother-in-law's home for a few hours every afternoon to read to her and prepare simple meals. These resources are a supplement to you; they won't replace you, but they can give you a few extra hours every week to regroup.
5. Enlist the help of your husband. Take the time to sit and talk with your husband about how overwhelmed you may be feeling; don't assume he knows. He may not comprehend the extent of the burden you've been carrying. Show him your list, tell him you're willing to work with him but that you

need *his* input, too. In turning some of the responsibility over to him, you're not only doing yourself a favor, but you're also giving him the opportunity to care for his own parents—and thereby playing a larger role in his extended family. If he truly was not aware of the duties you were carrying out, this new participation on his part may be a welcome role.

Speaking of the husband's role, there is often a hidden agenda in an in-law's escalating needs and often seemingly endless demands. Let's imagine your feelings as an elderly woman whose son is becoming more and more preoccupied with his work, handing over more and more of the family's contact with you to his wife. *She* drives you to the chiropractor; *she* calls the pharmacy when you don't understand when you're supposed to take your medicine; *she* picks up the mushrooms you need to have for your salad. You may adore your daughter-in-law, but it's only natural that you want to see your son more than once a month—especially if he lives nearby. So you gradually intensify your requests (often unconsciously), hoping that at some point your daughter-in-law will throw her hands up in disgust and that your son will be forced to step in.

Dora found herself in this position. Recently, she needed oral surgery, and her son Marvin, himself an oral surgeon, referred her to a close friend and colleague, one of the best in the business. As the day approached for the procedure to be done in the surgeon's office, Dora asked Marvin to drive her there. "Sorry, Mother," came the response, "I've got surgery to perform that same morning myself. But Alexis will take you."

Marvin's wife, Alexis, was perfectly willing to take Dora for her surgery. The older woman balked, becoming ornery and complaining that she didn't like the way Alexis drove, that she didn't like Alexis's car, that Alexis would get impatient with her, that

Alexis would bring the children and that would make Dora nervous. No matter what Marvin said, Dora was adamant. If her son wouldn't take her to the oral surgeon, she finally announced, she would hire a neighbor's daughter—at $100!—to drive her there and wait for her. At which point, feeling angry and totally manipulated, Marvin gave in and said he would take Dora, but not until there was an ugly scene with Alexis, and much bitterness all around.

Dora's needs were very real, but her tactics were regrettable. How much better it would have been if she had spoken quietly with her son, telling him how much she appreciated Alexis's kindnesses to her and her offer to drive Dora to the oral surgeon, but that she felt a very strong need to be with Marvin. Putting her feelings in these terms would have let Alexis know that Dora's quarrel was not with her, but with Marvin, and Marvin would have felt less put-upon and manipulated and more needed as a son.

For their part, Marvin and Alexis needed to be more sensitive and empathetic to how parents feel as they age. It's very hard to watch a beloved mother or father grow more dependent, especially if he or she is alone. Empathy—the quality of understanding how someone else is feeling in a particular situation—would have allowed Marvin and Alexis to understand that Dora was fearful of her impending surgery. They would have understood that the elderly woman was feeling vulnerable and that she wanted the person closest to her, her son, to be with her—and to *want* to be with her.

To smooth the way, Marvin might have said to his mother, "I know you are feeling scared, and I really want to stay with you, but I can't." This would have let her know that he was thinking of her, that he cared for her deeply and that he wanted to be by her side during her surgery.

Making Wishes Known Early On

Keeping communications open between the generations is as important now as at any point during a relationship—maybe even more so. There are issues on everyone's minds now that need to be expressed openly and without reservation: Who will take care of me if my Parkinson's disease gets worse and I can't feed myself? Who will pay if my mother-in-law has to go into a nursing home? What arrangements do I want to make for my funeral when the time comes? These are uncomfortable questions, and it's often easier for one generation or both to sweep them under the rug. Don't let that happen.

Often it's the younger family members who hide their heads in the sand, preferring not to face the fact that their parents are getting older. Husband or wife may not want to accept the reality of an incapacitated parent and may deny that the parent is diminished in any way. Eleanor, a client in her early seventies, told me that whenever she broached the subject of her will to her son and daughter-in-law, they turned aside the conversation with a hurried, "Oh, Mother, you'll be with us for many, many years," and quickly began to talk about the weather or the fact that the lawn needed mowing.

It's important for families to discuss these issues, painful as they are, so that when the time comes to place your father-in-law in a nursing home, or withhold heroic medical technology when your mother-in-law's cancer is so pervasive that no hope is left, *all* family members will be comfortable that the decisions have been well-thought-out and considered.

"I know you don't want to hear that I'm getting old," you might say, "but we need to talk about some things. I would feel more comfortable knowing you know my wishes about life support systems and how I want to be buried."

Nobody said it was going to be easy, but talking over your

wishes *now*, before disaster or disability strikes, is the best way to insure that your wishes will be met. You need to tell your daughter and son-in-law what arrangements you've already made—if any—for your funeral, where your cemetery plot is, where your important financial and health records are stored. If you have strong feelings about being on a life-support system if a catastrophic illness strikes, now is the time to share that information. Your feelings about residential care—from independent living to full-care nursing homes—should also be aired now. This type of sharing serves two purposes: It goes a long way toward seeing that your needs are met, and it takes the burden of making these gut-wrenching decisions off the shoulders of your children. Later, if siblings argue over whether Mom should be placed in a nursing home, they can recall that you said such a placement would be fine if you had input into the selection of the facility.

If you're like many people, you may fear that passing along this information for your children and in-laws is a sign of giving up your control. That couldn't be further from the truth. In fact, you're assuring yourself that you will *maintain* control in the event that you become incapacitated. If your wishes have already been made clear, your son and daughter-in-law have a strong base from which to begin planning for your care should the unthinkable happen.

Louise Fradkin, co-director of the national organization Children of Aging Parents, has some thought on how to approach the topic. Do it at a family meeting, she suggests, one at which all family members are actively involved, including the elderly person whose future is being debated. It might help to bring in an objective "third party" such as a social-worker, to help keep the proceedings flowing smoothly, or to informally designate a leader to keep things on track.

Early on in the meeting, establish the needs of the elderly person. Make a list—in writing—of what each family member will do in terms of offering time, money, or resources. For example, if you work part time, you can drive your father-in-law to his weekly card games at the senior center, or to do his food shopping. If your sister-in-law has more money than time, she can volunteer to pay for a cleaning service to come in once a week and tidy up his apartment. If your brother-in-law has neither time nor money, he can volunteer for a short-term project, perhaps making phone calls during his lunch hour to screen nursing homes if that need seems imminent.

A Bill of Rights for the Elderly

It doesn't appear in the Bill of Rights in so many words, but the right to live in dignity should be high on the list of rights accorded to the elderly. There is a tendency in this country to write off the senior citizen as a dotty old fool, as a mental incompetent, or as a senile hanger-on. It's almost a self-fulfilling prophecy. We expect them to be frail, sick, and forgetful—and they act accordingly. But you can break the cycle by following a few commonsense (and common-decency) rules.

1. Don't undermine the independence of the elderly. Nothing takes away a person's dignity faster than being stripped of decision-making powers. Don't automatically assume if your father-in-law has had a few episodes of forgetfulness or has become more bent-over with arthritis that he has lost the ability to make choices and pursue options for himself. Don't sell his beloved car without consulting him, just because he's bedridden and you know he'll never drive again. Don't make plans to move your mother-in-law into a nursing home without consulting her and taking her needs and her wishes into consideration.

   Keep in mind that a few episodes of forgetfulness do not necessarily mean that your in-law is sick, or on the brink of senility. A few tactful, carefully worded questions can help you determine just how firmly grounded in reality he or she is, and can give you a feel for his or her competence. "Are you remembering to take your medicine?" you might ask during a visit. "What did you have for dinner last night?" Included as part of a normal conversation, these questions won't be construed as a test of your in-law's mental capacities; rather, they can make her feel that you are genuinely interested in her.

2. Maintain physical contact. You may be afraid to touch your eighty-nine-year-old father-in-law because he looks so frail, but a gentle hand on the shoulder, or a brush of the lips across his cheek, can often do more than any medicine to enliven the outlook of the elderly. Older people need touch as much as younger people—often more. It sometimes takes an effort to put your arms around someone whose physical appearance may be less than appealing—let's face it, aging can ravage the face and body—but you need to get beyond that hesitation and provide that human touch your in-law so needs.
3. Keep up your in-laws' social contacts. If he is shut away in a nursing home, it's often easy to forget to include your father-in-law in holiday meals, birthday parties, and other celebrations. Don't. If she's housebound, bring her a special dinner the day (or day after) her grandson graduates from high school, or bring a friend she hasn't seen in a while over for a short visit. Plan outings that are appropriate—all their trips outside the house don't have to be to the doctor. Why not take your mother-in-law to the park to watch the children ride the carousel, or to an outdoor concert at a local arts center? How about a ride in the country to visit another relative?
4. Listen to what your in-law has to say. One of the most fre-

quent complaints I hear from elderly clients is, "Nobody listens to me." It takes real skill to *hear* what an aging mother-in-law has to say, rather than just listening with one part of your brain and nodding at what seems the appropriate time. But don't dismiss her words as mere chatter, her complaints as mere whining. Pay attention.

FACING HARD CHOICES

This very well might be the year someone in the family says, "Hey, we have to do something about Dad." It may be you, it may be your husband, it may be one of his brothers or sisters—or it may be Dad's doctor, who takes the family aside to suggest that some additional support systems need to be put into effect.

Chances are it won't come as a total surprise; you've been seeing little signs for some time now. There's your father-in-law's growing isolation—his friends have all died, or moved away to a warmer climate. You've noticed that his home is not laid out in a manner that's user-friendly for the elderly: It's hard for him to navigate the stairs to the basement, where the washer and dryer are located; or the apartment's one bathroom is on the second floor, thirteen steps up from the kitchen where he spends most of his time.

And you're concerned about his growing depression, his forgetfulness, his agitation over being alone. Increasingly, he is missing his morning dose of medicine because he forgets to take the pill, and you peek into his refrigerator to find it meagerly stocked—no milk, no fresh fruits or vegetables, no dairy items, just some skimpy scraps left over from a dinner his next-door neighbor sent over the night before.

Keep a sharp eye out when you visit your elderly in-law, asking yourself a series of questions that can guide your decision about when it's time to "do something about Dad." Among them:

Is he safe alone? Has he left pans burning on the stove until a fire was ignited? Does Dad wander—have neighbors told you they've seen him down the block, seemingly confused about how he got there . . . and how to get back? How much is Dad relying on others to get him through the day: to cook his meals and wash his clothes? Is he calling you constantly, complaining about being alone and not feeling well?

Who is most likely to notice any changes? It's the adult child or in-law who is living nearest, or the one who accompanies Dad to the doctor most often. Studies show that it is most apt to be a female relative who best has her finger on the pulse of what's going on.

Yes, it's time to do something about Dad. The question is: *what*? Arrange to have a health aide come by several times a week? Look into nursing homes? Have him move in with you? The choices are vast, the decision-making agonizing.

Exploring the Options

There is a wide variety of options and resources when it comes to care for the elderly, ranging from independent living to residence in a skilled nursing home that provides twenty-four-hour-a-day care. This continuum of care has many points, any of which might prove beneficial at any given time. Among them are support systems at home, adult day care, full-time care in a relative's home, group living in senior-citizen housing, and round-the-clock care in a nursing home.

How to decide on the right option? Start first by hooking up with a family-service agency—Catholic Family Services, for example, or a similar agency depending on your religious or ethnic affiliation—that has on its staff a gerontologist, or expert on aging. There are also state offices on aging whose staff members can fill you in on what facilities are available in your community and where to turn for help. Two other avenues would be geriatric-assessment agencies that are usually affiliated with an established nursing home, and independent social workers who serve as consultants to families dealing with the crisis of an elderly parent.

A Nursing Home—Or Your Home?

No matter how many times you've gone over the information, the conclusion is inescapable: Your mother-in-law cannot make it on her own anymore, and the choice is now between finding a satisfactory nursing home or bringing her into your home. Few decisions are as fraught with emotion—whatever path you take, there is a price to be paid, whether it be in terms of loss of privacy, or increased burden on your time, or the ever-present guilt that comes with placing a loved one in a facility.

Now is the time to do some real soul-searching—as well as some critical analyzing of external factors. There are several factors to consider before bringing an elderly person to live in your home.

1. What is the physical condition of my house? Are there stairs my father-in-law will have to navigate; is there only one bathroom that will have to accommodate one more person; will his arrival force one of my children out of his or her room?
2. How will the move affect the other members of my family? Will my teenage children feel they can no longer bring their friends over to listen to records and have noisy study sessions if my mother-in-law is occupying a bedroom on the same floor? Will I constantly be reminding my younger children, "Shhh, Grandma's sleeping"?
3. Are all family members out of the house all day in school or at jobs? If I'm working full time, the kids have afternoon activities and my husband hasn't made it home from the

office for dinner in six years, am I really doing my father-in-law any service by bringing him into a house where he'll be alone all day?

4. How mentally and physically competent is my in-law? Does his mind wander, so he thinks that I'm his late wife . . . or his mother? Does he confuse day and night—a common problem among the very old—so that he is awake and restless while the rest of my family is trying to sleep? Is he sensitive to noise and/or light, so that I will have to alter household patterns?
5. Am I physically capable of taking care of an invalid—and do I really know what's involved in this type of responsibility? Do I have the sheer physical strength to transfer my 140-pound mother-in-law from bed to toilet, from wheelchair to bed? To provide round-the-clock bedpan service and meals? To be on call all hours of the day and night?

You've considered all these questions and their ramifications openly and honestly, and you've decided—or, as is most often the case, your husband has decided—to bring Mother into the house. But before you do, it's incumbent upon you, the daughter-in-law, to do one more thing. Sit down and write out a detailed job description, listing everything—and I mean *everything*—that will be expected of you. From keeping her company and answering the telephone calls she gets to preparing her meals, running interference with your teenage sons, and washing three extra loads a week.

When you've finished, take that written list to a family meeting—it will serve as your evidence before the court, so to speak. It's very possible that your husband never really took the time to realize just what was involved in caring for his mother. Your list—your documentation—removes the issue from the realm of "You're not being nice to my mother" and puts it in the realm of "Maybe we *would* be biting off more than we can chew."

Keep in mind, too, that if you've had a stormy relationship with this woman, it's only going to get stormier if she moves in with you. Age tends to exacerbate quirks and eccentricities, and it exaggerates small grievances until they turn into yawning caverns. When you're living together, old wounds can open up again, old hurts can surface. If she's always harped on what she sees as your meager housekeeping skills, she's not suddenly going to begin singing your praises. If she's always resented the fact that you work outside the home, your new living arrangements are only going to fuel her complaints.

Once you have made the decision to move your mother-in-law into your home, be prepared for the emotional changes that can accompany such a move, and the traps that all family members can fall into under these new, unfamiliar arrangements. There is likely to be competition between the two women suddenly thrust into one home; there may be jockeying for control of decision-making, and there is almost definitely going to be tension caused by people rubbing up against each other in the confines of your home's four walls—whether you live in a three-room apartment or a thirty-two-room mansion.

Eva was seventy-two, a robust seventy-two, but someone whose friends had one by one moved to Florida, leaving her increasingly isolated and alone. When Eva's son, Peter, and his wife, Lynne, visited, they noted with some alarm that the older woman, a widow, had almost no one left in the neighborhood to call in case of emergency, and that her only contact on a daily basis was with the mailman making his rounds. It took some persuading on his part, but Peter convinced his mother to come live with his family.

The two women had never had a close relationship. Over the twenty-two years Lynne had been married to Peter, she and Eva had maintained some congeniality, but no real warmth. In fact, Peter hadn't got along well with Eva, either—son and mother fought constantly over her unceasing criticism. But as the oldest boy in the family—Peter had three younger brothers—he was determined to "do the right thing." So Eva came to stay, bringing her women's magazines, her quilting, and her crossword puzzles.

Almost as soon as she began to settle in, the fights began. Every time Lynne said something—anything—to Peter, his mother would butt in, offering her two cents. Invariably, she sided with Lynne (Eva wasn't crazy; she didn't want to threaten her newfound comfortable home), and harped on Peter's alleged shortcomings. Now, the couple was fighting more and more, egged on by Eva. Every time they tried to conduct a civil conversation, Eva would intrude. Lynne was already feeling put-upon because she'd had this extra burden thrust upon her, Peter was chafing over his mother's endless attacks, the teenage children were picking up on the hostility. Everyone was miserable.

The solution to a sticky situation like this lies in setting some limits to allow both the couple and the mother-in-law space and privacy—mental, emotional, and physical privacy.

If you're caught in the same trap as Lynne and Peter, you must let your in-law know that you need private time, not just for romance but also for down-to-earth talks, for day-to-day catching-up, even for fights. No one likes to conduct personal business in a store window, but that's just what was happening in Peter and Lynne's case. Faced with this situation, you and your husband have to talk with your elderly houseguest *together*. Not just you, so you're the heavy, but as a couple. The conversation could go something like this: "Mother, we need to have some time alone. If you'd like, we can set up the spare television in your room, so you can watch your favorite shows. Or we'll be glad to pick up some books or magazines for you. But we do need some time by ourselves."

Another solution would be to suggest that your mother-in-law might like to take a brief "vacation" from you, and visit one of her other children for a short while. This gives both you and her a breather, and allows you almost to start anew when she returns.

As important as it was years ago, when you may have moved into *her* house, it's even more essential now to set up some elementary house rules by which everyone agrees to abide. Ideally, these should be "negotiated" even before your in-law moves in, but in reality it's never too late to set up some guidelines. At a family meeting you might draw up a list that addresses some of these issues:

1. Laundry Rules: Who's in charge here? Does the son or the daughter-in-law do communal washes for everyone, or does each family member—including Grandma—wash his or her clothes? If it's the latter, you might need to work out a schedule for use of the washing machine and the dryer, so there's no quarrel over whose turn it is.
2. Bathroom Use: If three people have to be out of the house by 8:00 A.M., it's fair to ask anyone who doesn't have to watch the clock to take his or her shower in the evening. It's also reasonable to expect each person to clean up after himself or herself.
3. Kitchen Control: The ancient Chinese symbol for "trouble" is two women under one roof. The modern version is a mother-in-law and a daughter-in-law in one kitchen. This is a touchy subject, often best handled by assigning days or meals to a particular individual: Daughter-in-law makes dinner Monday, Wednesday, and Friday; mother-in-law makes dinner Tuesday and Sunday; son makes dinner Thursday and Saturday.
4. Money Matters: This is a really sticky issue, best handled in an up-front and honest manner. Who's going to pay for food,

telephone, utilities? Will these be shared by the "guest" and the homeowners, or borne solely by the homeowners? If costs are to be shouldered equally, you'll need to work out the logistics early on—who pays for what, when, and how much?

My Apple Pie Is Better than Your Apple Pie

You're already feeling intruded upon, put out, overly burdened. All you need is this: Your mother-in-law is competing with you for her son's attention—and for the role of mistress of the house. It can be subtle or it can be blatant ("Philip doesn't like your pot roast as well as he likes mine"; "Philip likes the way I iron his shirts better.") The best response to this is often no response at all: Just don't play into it. It's like a tug-of-war—if one person lets go, the game is over. You can't play tug-of-war with yourself. The same applies to this type of competition on the home front.

It often helps the younger person in the relationship to understand *why* her mother-in-law is waging this subtle "war." Remember, your in-law has probably lost her husband, her own home, her role as a parent, and—perhaps most painfully—her sense of control over her life. This one-upmanship, this jockeying for her son's attention, may be her unconscious attempt to win back something to replace what she has lost.

Your best bet is refusing to be drawn in. Don't engage in verbal battle with her over whose pie is the tastiest, whose housekeeping the most meticulous. Chances are the jousting won't cease overnight, but it probably will recede a little. Your mother-in-law is not going to change magically, but the situation is less volatile if you're not rising to the bait.

Who's in Charge Here?

"You need to get more fiber into your diet."
"Don't tell me what I need to eat."
"It's too hot for you to go out today."
"Don't tell me when I can go out and when I can't."

Molly, an active widow of seventy-eight who loved going to the opera and to art galleries, suffered a minor stroke that left her dragging her right leg and suffering some loss of the use of her right hand. Her son, Gordon, and his wife, Betsy, decided to bring her home with them after she was released from the hospital. Still somewhat dazed by what had happened to her, but determined to get fully back on her feet, Molly accepted the kids' hospitality gratefully.

In the first few weeks, Betsy, an outgoing and friendly homemaker, proved to be a superb host and nurse. She cooked all of Molly's favorite meals, took her to physical-therapy sessions at the hospital, reminded her when to take her pills. But as she began to feel stronger and more like her old self, Molly started resenting her daughter-in-law's "orders": "Mom, you can't walk those steps; they're too steep for you." "Mother, you need to put on a heavier sweater if you're going to sit on the porch." Even worse, when Molly made any attempt to contribute to the running of the household—setting the table for dinner, for example, or doing a small load of washing—Betsy yelled at her, reminding Molly that she had been out of the hospital less than a month, and that she was still weak from the stroke. The situation only got worse as Molly continued to improve, to the point where the two women were barely civil to each other.

The question is a simple one: Who make the decisions here?

The ongoing struggle of wills when a young person is playing host to an older one can escalate until it encompasses every facet of life: what the elderly person should eat and wear, what company she should have, what time she should take her medicine.

Often, the battle over decision-making begins when your in-law first moves in with you. She may be debilitated from a stroke or a heart attack, she may still be in shock from the loss of her husband, she may be reeling from the life changes that have so suddenly been thrust upon her. During a crisis like this, a person's decision-making ability can be severely impaired, so she may accept—even welcome—a take-charge attitude. It may be soothing for her to know she doesn't have to remember when to take her pills, or have to decide what to have for dinner when even such a minor decision looms large.

But as she slowly gets back on her feet, the feeling of being soothed may evolve into a feeling of being smothered. By then, though, the patterns may be so firmly established, that you, as the daughter-in-law, feel you need to continue making the decisions for the in-law you still see as incapacitated. When she's ready to take back control, you're unwilling to relinquish it.

At this point, you must understand the battle of wills that is being waged and back off from it. Be alert to signs that your mother-in-law is ready to take back the reins. Is she chafing when you dole out her medicine? Does she resent it when you tell her not to walk to the mailbox because it's too far and she'll get tired? Remember that she's the best judge of what she can and cannot do—and it's your job to respect that judgment.

If you're the mother-in-law facing this loss of control, stand your ground. Find certain things you *can* control: Bring your medicine into your room and take it on your own. Call the doctor yourself if you have a question about your health, rather than depending on your daughter-in-law to do it. Remind her gently, rather than antagonistically, that you are an adult, that you appreciate her care and her concern, but that you can make decisions very competently, thank you.

The Nursing-Home Option

Opting to place an elderly parent or in-law in a nursing home can be one of the most wrenching and guilt-producing decisions a couple can make. Every emotion known to mankind is aroused—anger, loss, fear, sadness, guilt—in all the parties involved. You have to place Mom in a nursing home, but you know how much Mom treasures her independence; how much she values taking a bath when *she* wants to, reading long into the night when *she* wants to, eating the meals *she* has prepared for herself. So you agonize over the decision.

This is sometimes a juncture where families wind up divided. Suppose you are convinced that your husband's dad—who has been staying with you—needs to go into a home, and your brothers- and sisters-in-law do not agree? Your first action would be to call a family meeting, letting everyone else know what the situation is and in what areas you are feeling overwhelmed: you no longer have the ability to lift Dad on and off the bedpan four or five times a day; you are alarmed at his decreasing mental acuity; you have no time whatsoever to spend with your own children.

It's my experience with families that most siblings will agree on the need for a placement once these issues are dealt with openly and honestly. I have also found that most are willing to contribute in some way—if not with the physical care, at least with the financial burden.

Once the decision has been reached, you and your husband *together* should let his mother or father know that the nursing-home option is being explored, so neither of you becomes the "bad guy"—the one who takes the blame for "putting me away." You should also discuss it with your in-law *after* you've finished any arguments you and your husband may have had, so as not to draw the older person into the battle.

Once you've found a pleasant and pleasing nursing home, and your in-law has settled in, what's the best policy for visiting him or her there? Here are some simple guidelines:

1. Shorter, more frequent visits are more welcome than longer, less frequent visits. Your aging relative, often weakened by illness, will appreciate seeing you several times a week for an hour more than once a month for three or four hours. The shorter visits are less tiring and demanding; the more frequent visits give your in-law something to look forward to.
2. Make the visits convenient for both of you. If you resent time that you're giving up—time you feel should have been spent finishing a report for your boss or watching your daughter's soccer practice—your in-law is going to sense it. And the visit will be unpleasant for both of you.
3. Encourage your children to visit. Be willing to take them, prepare them the first time for what they are going to see. If they're used to seeing their grandfather as a strong, independent rock, let them know of the changes aging has wrought, and describe the surroundings in which they will see him.
4. Realize that your mother-in-law might regard you "the enemy" if she thinks you had a hand in putting her into the home. It's always easier to blame "the stranger" for unpleasantness, especially if she has done so all her life. This is her way of coping. It will help you to get reassurance from other family members that you did not "do this" to your mother-in-law unilaterally; that everyone shared in the decision. If your husband's mother accuses you bitterly of "abandoning her," point out gently and calmly that everyone in the family

thinks that this is the best place for her, and that you all still care for her and want her to be safe and comfortable.

5. Encourage your husband to visit his parent alone. Take the burden off yourself by realizing that you don't have to accompany him every time he makes the trip. Furthermore, if he is not visiting her as much as you think is appropriate, don't feel you have to go to pick up the slack. You don't have to replace him—indeed, you can't. You can't go as his replacement; you can only go as a daughter-in-law.

Summing Up

A middle-aged woman spoke to me recently about her son's impending wedding. "This young woman is my insurance policy for when I get old," she said of her future daughter-in-law. "My son loves me, but I know she'll be the one to take care of me when I get old."

Her bittersweet comment sums up the reality of these later years. It speaks to the fear of growing old and infirm, and of the role many daughters-in-law will have thrust upon them. From my clients shouldering this burden, I hear frustration over the weight of the responsibility, not just the physical, but also the emotional. "I didn't like her all along, and now I'm faced with taking care of her," they say. "I feel as though there was an unspoken battle between me and my mother-in-law, and my husband chose his mother over me. How can I handle that?"

Be open to all the channels of help that are out there—including friends who are going through the same things, support groups, maybe a counselor who can help you sort it all out. Your goal is to sort out these feelings, and to be able to put your anger and your frustration into perspective while easing the burden on your time and your psyche.

It's no easier if you're the elderly person who has suddenly found himself or herself needy and dependent after a lifetime of independence and strength. In a society that teaches us to be more guarded with strangers, not let our defenses down, this new role can feel humiliating and depressing. Even though you may have known your daughter-in-law for twenty years or more, she's still not a blood relative, and your increasing need to lean on her feels demeaning.

What this period calls for on everyone's part is understanding and tact, and an ability to make the best of a trying situation. The increased social services and support groups available for the aged make this almost a golden age compared with the wasteland of fifty years ago. As the population ages, more and more of these services will be put into place. So there are many ways to lessen the burden of caring for an elderly in-law. Try to plug into some of these; be willing to share the responsibility. Remember, martyrdom is a nonpaying job.

CHAPTER EIGHT

When Divorce and Widowhood Change the Picture

Friends and family told Marcy she was making a mistake marrying Raymond—that at twenty-one they were both way too young to tie the knot—but the tall, soft-spoken Marcy was passionately in love with Raymond, who had the strong sense of self-confidence that she lacked. Fifteen years and two kids later, Marcy sadly concluded that everybody else had been right. Husband and wife had grown in separate directions over the past decade and a half. While Raymond was content with his middle-management job at a local bank, Marcy yearned for new and exciting vistas. Going back to school to get her degree in sociology only made things worse. Now, the couple was fighting day and night—Marcy resentful because Raymond wasn't chipping in and carrying his share of the workload at home, Raymond bewildered and bitter that the quiet and devoted girl he had married fifteen years earlier was changing before his very eyes.

Something else was changing: Marcy's relationship with her mother-in-law, Sherry. As the young couple slouched closer and closer toward divorce, the amicable bonds between the two women were slowly unraveling. They had been on solid terms; Marcy depended on Sherry for supplementary childcare when she couldn't make other arrangements, and Sherry had been generous with gifts of time and money. They respected each other. When Marcy announced she was going back to school, her mother-in-law was cautious—although she approved of the younger woman's drive for education, she was nervous about the effect her schoolwork would have on the marriage. Sherry kept quiet, not wanting to jeopardize the relationship the women had built over the years.

At the onset of the marital problems, Marcy used her mother-in-law as a sounding board, complaining of Raymond's inflexibility about his schedule and his unwillingness to share in housekeeping, cooking, and marketing chores. As it grew more apparent that divorce was inevitable, it became harder for Sherry to keep listening to Marcy's complaints without some bitterness of her own. She saw that Raymond was hurting, and felt angry and resentful at Marcy for the pain she was causing. She also worried about the effects of a divorce on her grandchildren.

As time went on, the two women began phoning each other less and less. When they did talk, Sherry made it clear that she didn't want to hear Marcy's gripes. By the same token, when Sherry tried to discuss the impact of the tense situation on the grandchildren, Marcy was withdrawn and cold, and discouraged any further conversation.

"I feel as though I'm going to lose my grandchildren," a depressed and anxious Sherry said to me during a counseling session. "I've already lost my daughter-in-law, and my son is miserable and unhappy. What am I supposed to be doing here? What's my role?"

Different Events, Same Results

Although they are two very different life events, divorce and the death of a spouse have a surprisingly similar impact on the family. Both disrupt the established links between generations. Both change the nature of the support systems you have got used to. Not only do you lose a spouse, but in the case of divorce, for example, you may also lose friends who take your ex's side; in instances when your spouse has died, you may also lose contact with *his* friends as well.

In addition, both divorce and death create the need for individuals to renegotiate existing relationships.

In this chapter, we'll explore ways to renegotiate your in-law ties—and, in some cases, to even make them stronger. We'll talk about the demands that life-changing events place on in-law relation, and how to meet those demands. We'll share ideas for getting through the tough times together—breaking the news of an upcoming divorce, for example, or fighting over who chooses the clergyperson when a husband/son has died—and suggest ways you can remain on cordial terms after the crisis.

Till Divorce Do Us Part

When you marry a man, you are not marrying just him but also his entire family. So, too, when you divorce, you are divorcing an entire family. The ripple effect from the breakup of a marriage spreads to his mother, his father, his siblings, and possibly even his grandparents, if they are still alive.

When marital bliss begins to turn to marital stress, relationships that have evolved over years take on a new slant. In-laws who were close to both spouses may suddenly find themselves siding with one or the other, often casting one in the role of villain and the other in the role of victim. A wife carrying a ton of bitterness against her husband might widen that emotion to include her husband's parents—after all, she reasons, they raised him, didn't they? Furthermore, a husband and wife who were fairly open and honest with their parents for years might gradually turn reclusive and reticent when problems crop up—leaving the older generation feeling left out and able to imagine only the worst.

As it was in the very early stages of marriage, and in the months and years that followed, limit-setting on the part of all family members is still the key to working through this difficult period. There has to be a renegotiation of time-sharing and information-sharing, with all parties understanding clearly their role in the new family constellation. This is especially true when youngsters are involved, and grandparents face the very real risk of losing access to their beloved grandchildren.

What is your role as an in-law when you realize that your son or daughter's marriage is in trouble? Like Sherry, you will most likely experience a wide range of emotions, almost all of them negative: anguish, resentment, worry, uncertainty, pain for your child and for the children of your child. There are some concrete steps you can take to make the situation a little more tolerable for yourself—and for everyone involved.

Helpful Hints for In-laws Whose Kids Are Divorcing

1. Remain neutral. This is tough but essential, even if you have definite feelings about who's in the wrong here. While you're listening to your son or daughter complain and moan about his or her spouse, remember that while the pain is definitely

there, not all marital difficulties end in divorce. If you have fueled the fire during this time of tension by heaping verbal abuse on your in-law, and the couple works things out after all, you're going to be resented at best, or possibly completely cut off from the younger couple at worst.

2. Don't oversympathize. It's tremendously difficult to watch your child suffer, and the desire is strong to clasp him to your bosom and say, "Oh, you poor baby—how can she do this to you?" That's a sure way to hasten the demise of the marriage or, again, to alienate your child if the marriage survives.
3. Listen well. Be a good listener without telling either party what to do. Try to be understanding of everyone's feelings, but avoid stepping in and taking charge. When Raymond complained to Sherry that Marcy never made him dinner anymore because of her heavy class load, Sherry might have responded, "It sounds as though you're questioning Marcy's feelings for you," rather than rushing over to make dinner herself, or egging Raymond on by saying, "She's a rotten wife. She should be there for you."
4. Don't gossip. Restrain yourself from talking to the rest of the family about the couple's marital problems; that's no one's business but theirs. Let the couple know that you will respect their confidentiality, and then make sure you do so.
5. Don't try to be a marriage counselor. If your son and daughter-in-law try to press you into this role, your best bet is to encourage them to seek help from a professional family therapist, someone with the training needed to guide them through the rocky terrain—and the objectivity needed to remain neutral. If you're asked for specific information and have the answers, fine, but don't get too involved. A professional has considerably less at stake here personally; furthermore, he or she is not likely to become the target later on if the marriage ultimately fails.

If your a divorcing couple, what can you do to keep your in-laws from interfering at this very difficult time of your life? It's one of mankind's strongest instincts to offer advice—and with today's high rate of separation and divorce, chances are your spouse's parents might have gone through similar hard times. If so, it's a good bet that they will feel compelled to share their experiences with you. At this point, saying to them something like this might help: "Mom, Dad, I know your marriage had its rocky moments, and you may have gone through a painful divorce, but Mitch's and my problems are different from yours and we need to work this out by ourselves." This approach lets your in-laws (or your parents, if they're the ones you're dealing with) know that you appreciate their concerns; that although their problems may have been similar, your life experiences are considerably different from theirs, and that you're on top of things as much as you can be.

Don't kid yourself into thinking that your parents and his don't suspect or know what's going on. For the most part, they will be pretty attuned to what's happening if they have regular contact with you. They may begin to cross-examine you before you're ready to share information with them. You will need to work out some strategy for protecting yourself from in-laws hungry for information while at the same time not hurting them unnecessarily by withholding important facts.

Often, if you're already in marital or family counseling, your therapist can act as a "shield" of sorts. When faced with a question you're not prepared to answer, have an explanation ready: "We talk a lot about this issue in counseling, and we don't feel comfortable talking about it with anybody else." Most parents, unless they're incredibly intrusive, will respect that.

If the questions persist, however, it might help to look at it this way: Isn't it nice to know they care so much, that they are open to discussion and willing to serve as a sounding board?

Is there a danger in sharing *too much* information? Yes, and it takes several forms. First of all, dumping a lot of negative feelings on the older generation can leave them feeling depressed and disappointed in your and your spouse. Freely hurling accusations in front of them, charging your partner with the most heinous of marital crimes, puts a pretty hefty burden on your partner's parents. If you then proceed to patch things up, your parents and in-laws are left with a lot of excess emotion that they won't know what to do with.

Another pattern to avoid is allowing your parents and his—as well as sisters, brothers, and cousins—to fan the embers when your marriage is under fire. If allowed to voice their opinions, they may actually create a deeper rift between you and your husband than would exist if you were left alone to work things out.

Siblings-in-law can often offer a great deal of support as you go through the pain and hurt of divorce and separation. Often they can remain more objective and open to hearing both sides of an issue—if it's their brother involved in the marital dispute, for example, they've probably been engaged in some degree of sibling rivalry since infancy. But fraternal ties don't always work to everyone's advantage, as Cliff and Adrienne found out.

Madeline, a thirtyish photographer who describes herself as "single and looking," has secretly been jealous of her sister-in-law, Adrienne, for years. Although they are roughly the same age, Adrienne has been married to Cliff, Madeline's brother, for six years. They have two charming daughters, a rambling suburban ranch house, and a full social life. Adrienne's got it made, Madeline thought. That was, until marital stresses turned into marital strife, and Adrienne and Cliff began growing apart.

Soon Cliff started sharing his discontent with his sister, dropping hints that all was not well and seeking support. He got it all right—Madeline was quick to pick up on Cliff's criticism of his wife . . . and to carry it further. "I never liked her," Madeline confided to her brother. "She's spoiled, she doesn't appreciate you, and she takes you for granted. I always thought you could do better."

What Madeline was doing fueled the fires between husband and wife, and I told them so during marital counseling. "You need to separate her jealousy from your own relationship. You have to set boundaries—not letting other people into your personal fight," I told Cliff and Adrienne. "Cliff, you have to tell your sister that you don't want to hear her gripes about your wife. Going to her for support is different from listening to her criticisms."

As for Madeline, she need to recognize that in setting herself up so clearly as Adrienne's adversary, she is jeopardizing her relationship with her two nieces. As the potential custodial parent, her sister-in-law easily could limit Madeline's visits to the two little girls—or, at the very least, Adrienne can influence how her daughters feel about their aunt Madeline. Either way, Madeline stands to lose.

What you need to do at this point is keep the boundaries of your relationship with your in-laws even more firmly established than when things were going smoothly. You may even have to spend less time with your in-laws. You may have to insist on a vacation from information-sharing, just until you get over the rough parts, or until things get so bad that a divorce is inevitable. This is a tough stance to take, especially if you need emotional support from your parents and his parents at a particularly painful period in your life. It's a matter of balance: offer enough information to satisfy the older couple's needs, and little enough to allow you to maintain your privacy.

SHARING THE BAD NEWS

Unlike breaking the news that you are going to get married or that you are going to make them grandparents, telling your parents and in-laws that you and your spouse are going to get a divorce is painful and awkward. It's not something most parents have looked forward to most of their lives. Some parents may have already picked up on the signs, overhearing sharp words you and your husband have hissed at each other, or feeling the heavy tension of silent anger in a household. On the other hand, if they are living some distance away and see you only infrequently, or if you have taken great pains to disguise your marital battling, the news is going to be a bitter shock.

At what point do they need to know what's going on? It's a very arbitrary decision, but certainly if a separation or divorce seems inevitable—and definitely if there are children involved—the older generation has a right to know what's coming.

Is there a right way or a wrong way to break the news? I encourage each spouse to approach his or her parents separately to let them know the status of the marriage. Then, in gentle terms and sharing only as much as you are comfortable with sharing, let them know that you and Karen have separated, that you are staying at a friend's house temporarily, and that you will do everything you can to make sure they will get to see their grandchildren.

The reaction is likely to be . . . unpredictable. Some couples come to me and say their parents reacted to the news with tears, but that they immediately offered their support and their unconditional love: "We're here if you need us" is the message they get. Some report that they were barraged with questions: "How long has this been going on?" "Whose fault is it?" "Have you seen a marriage counselor?" Others say the announcement was greeted with shrieks of anguish and with chest-beating: "Why are you doing this to me?" comes the accusation. "What did I do wrong as a parent? Where did I go wrong?"

When accusations are hurled at you, how should you respond? You have to make it clear up-front that the divorce is between *you* and *your spouse*; the problems is yours, not theirs. Tell them you are not divorcing as a personal affront to them, or to get back at them for anything. Tell them that as painful as the situation may be to *them*, it's doubly hard for *you*.

Renegotiating the Ties

Shelly, a librarian, and Sean, a college English teacher, found after fifteen years of marriage that it wasn't working. They'd had a trial separation, they'd tried counseling, they'd talked desultorily about staying together for the sake of the kids, ten-year-old Abbie, and twelve-year-old Christie, but the end was clearly in sight. Shelly and her soon-to-be-ex-mother-in-law had never got along very well; Shelly saw Maryjane as cold and aloof, Maryjane saw her daughter-in-law as shy, timid, and hard to approach.

In fact, Shelly and Sean had fought often about Maryjane. In loud and bitter arguments, Sean would accuse his wife of ignoring his mother, yelling at her, ""Why don't you talk to her more? Why don't you ever call her? My brother Lou's wife calls her all the time." When the marriage finally broke up, there were lots of reasons, but Shelly's relationship with Maryjane played a definite role.

Once Sean moved out, Shelly found herself feeling very alone. Ironically, the first holiday that rolled around was Mother's Day, which left the newly single mother feeling very vulnerable and depressed. On a whim—and also because she wanted to maintain some ties between her children and their grandmother—Shelly decided to take Cristie and Abbie to visit Maryjane.

The visit, much to Shelly's amazement, went extremely well.

The older woman was surprised, appreciative, and welcoming. "I felt incredibly relaxed in her presence for the first time in 15 years!" Shelly said. "You know why? Because it was *my* decision to go see her, with no pressure from Sean." The two women chatted about the children, how they were faring with the separation. They talked about the latest Stephen King thriller, the latest Michael Douglas movie, the newest French restaurant in town. What they didn't talk about, through unspoken agreement, was Sean—a wise decision.

Shelly continued to visit Maryjane, on her own terms and only when *she* wanted to. She found she enjoyed going to the older woman's home. What before had been a burden was now a joy, as she and her ex-mother-in-law explored literature, art, and music together in lively conversations. Moreover, Shelly watched gratefully as her daughters became even closer than they had been before to their grandmother—a tie the younger woman did all she could to encourage.

"What a pity this couldn't have happened *before* the divorce," Shelly said. "I'm closer now to Maryjane than I ever was in fifteen years of marriage."

A Relationship Redefined

That Shelly could report such a dramatic change is no coincidence. She and her former mother-in-law had in effect redefined their relationship. They had stopped seeing each other in stereotypical roles and begun appreciating each other as individuals.

Sudden alliances don't always follow a divorce, of course. If you've had an extremely poor or particularly hostile relationship, you probably won't warm up to each other once the marriage is over. If your father-in-law or mother-in-law has taken sides in the battles that preceded the split—if your father-in-law, for example, consistently tried to turn your husband away from you—

you're not likely to become bosom buddies afterward. Also, if you're truly unable to separate the anger you bear toward your spouse from your feelings about his family, and all you want to do is wash your hands of the entire bunch of them—then, no, you're not suddenly going to become best friends with your mother-in-law.

In many cases, both generations will find it to their advantage to nurture the ties between them: the mother-in-law because it helps guarantee that she will have access to her grandchildren, and the daughter-in-law because her in-laws can provide a support system and a sense of extended family when her own family is breaking up.

It is essential to lay the groundwork for future good relations during the separation and the divorce proceedings. You, as the mother-in-law, have to realize anew that taking sides during the quarrels and tension can only ricochet later. You also have to make it clear to your daughter-in-law that you want to keep the tie strong, and that visits to you will not be an exercise in self-defense for her. Let her know that you won't use her visits to lobby for your son, and that you won't clutter your time together with accusations that she sabotaged the marriage. You may feel this way inside, but it's wiser to *keep* it inside—remember, the stakes may be your grandchildren.

You must also make a conscious effort to separate your disappointment over your child's failed marriage from your feelings toward your daughter-in-law. Remember, it takes two to make a marriage—and it takes two to break a marriage. As disappointed and hurt as you are that Gerald and Hillary couldn't make it work, chances are it's not only *Hillary's* fault. It may be hard to distribute the blame equally, but you can rest assured that both parties probably had an equal part in writing finis to the marriage.

One way to continue the relationship you have with your daughter-in-law is by offering her non-judgmental help—maybe financial, maybe in terms of childcare, maybe just by being there. This requires a high degree of objectivity, mutual respect, and geographical proximity—and a deep pocketbook wouldn't hurt, either. I know many a grandmother who won her daughter-in-law's heart by helping out financially—being there spring and fall to provide a child's wardrobe, or buying extra little luxuries such as a large stuffed rabbit at Easter or a junior high school dinner out.

What can a daughter-in-law do to keep the lines of communication open and the relationship friendly—and why bother at all? First of all, at a time when your family life is falling apart, it can be a source of comfort to have a ready-made family standing nearby, even if it *is* your husband's family. Especially if your own mother and father live far away—or if they are deceased—you may find you need the solid reliability and wisdom of a surrogate parent to help get you through the searing pain and loneliness that often accompany a divorce. From a purely practical perspective, also, an extra pair of hands can be a blessing in those early months of single parenthood, when you're still new to juggling the often-conflicting demands of career, home, and family. Knowing you can count on Grandpa to pick Marla up at ballet lessons after school and Grandma to run Jared to the pediatrician can provide some relief to a mind teeming with deadlines, demands, and calls for your time.

Then, too, a loving father-in-law or brother-in-law can be helpful as a male role model for your children, especially if their father has left for parts unknown. A day at the zoo or a night at the movies with Uncle Jeffrey can be a special treat to a little boy who hasn't seen his daddy in a month.

The bottom line is that children who have been buffeted by the winds of an acrimonious divorce crave the comfort of being part of an extended family. They need to know that they belong to something that endures and are part of an extended family unit that accepts them and loves them unconditionally, just for who they are. That's the best motivation I can offer for a daughter-in-law to stay close to her in-laws after the divorce. Don't give unnecessary pain to youngsters who are already grieving over the loss of something precious to them: the stability of their home life.

How can you keep the ties tied? You have to be willing to take a risk, as Shelly did when she brought her children to visit Maryjane on Mother's Day, with no idea of how she'd be received. It took a certain amount of courage to make that first move—and then to follow up with subsequent visits. For Shelly, the risk was worth it, because she was feeling a strong need to connect with family on a particularly family-oriented day.

You, like your mother-in-law, have to separate your feelings toward her from the bitterness and anger you feel toward your ex. There's nothing more satisfying than promising yourself during that last heated battle that you'll never have to see him or his blasted family again as long as you live. In the end, you may only be hurting yourself (and, tragically, your children) if you take this path. It may be hard to realize now, in the heat of your anger, but your relationship with your mother-in-law might be a source of comfort and support when you're struggling to make it on your own. So make that vow to wash your hands of her if you must—but keep it to yourself. You may well change your mind down the road.

There's one more thing you as a daughter-in-law have to keep in mind during these rocky and demanding times. Although you may feel an overwhelming urge to blame your mother-in-law for the failure of your marriage, don't do it. Striking out in times of pain and bewilderment is a natural human reaction, and in your ex-husband's mother you have what looks like the perfect target. *She* raised him, didn't she? She passed down values to him, didn't she?—if he's stubborn and stingy and cold, it's *her* fault, isn't it? If he refused to pick up after himself and left the bathroom looking as though Hurricane Hugo had just passed through—well, didn't he learn these ways at his mother's knee?

It's awfully tempting to adopt this way of thinking, but not particularly helpful. Not only is this rationale too facile, it's also probably unjustified. There comes a point at which a person takes charge of his or her life—your husband acted the way he did on his own volition, not just because his Mommy never forced him to pick up his socks. Worst of all, "punishing" your mother-in-law for your husband's sins is a misdirected action that ultimately hurts the people who are most vulnerable: your children.

Maintaining Ties with the Grandchildren

Melissa's parents divorced when she was just two. Now a leggy, long-haired teenager of fifteen with some leftover baby pudginess, she was still paying the price. Jack and Sybil, her parents, had engaged in a nasty custody battle that raged on for eight years—and even then didn't have a peaceful resolution. Although Sybil had had custody for the past five years, and Jack had clear visitation rights (he saw his daughter twice a month, half of each summer and alternate Christmases and Thanksgivings), the disgruntled father kept going back to court to challenge the status quo. Meanwhile, ex-husband and ex-wife were barely civil toward each other; both were remarried, but the bitterness and hurt remained.

When it was Jack's turn to see Melissa, he drove 150 miles each way from his upstate New York home to Philadelphia to pick up his daughter. Sybil made things as difficult as possible by not allowing her daughter to take the train to visit her father and her grandparents, who lived in the same town. Tom and Marian,

Jake's parents, worked hard to build a close and warm relationship with Melissa, and watched the custody wars with dismay and concern. To keep the avenues of communications as open as possible, the older couple told Melissa she could call them whenever she wanted to, collect.

As their granddaughter approached sixteen, Tom and Marian cooked up a surprise for her: a trip, with them, to London, Paris, and Amsterdam. It was a dream come true for Melissa, who had thrown herself into French literature with a passion since she was twelve.

The promised trip quickly turned into a nightmare when it fueled the animosity between Melissa's parents. Neither adult was against the trip, mind you, but both took the position *not on my time, you don't.*

"They've taken what should have been a wonderful, exciting birthday for me and turned it into something sour," the pretty teenager said. "They're fighting over me again, but sometimes I think it's not because they want *me*, but because they want to get even with *each other*. But the bottom line is, I lose every time. And so do my grandmother and grandfather."

Melissa was unusually astute for a youth of fifteen, but it doesn't take an Einstein to recognize that the most common victims in a nasty divorce are the children, and the least visible are the grandparents. Often a husband or wife is so bitter and so angry at a spouse that he or she will lash out in any way possible—including denying a spouse's parents access to the grandchildren. "I'll get back at that louse Dave" is the attitude. "There's no way I'll let his parents *near* Jill and Erica."

Fortunately, the law has a remedy for this type of situation. Since 1985, grandparents who are denied permission to visit their grandchildren have had legal recourse in most states under the U.S. Custody Act. The legislation is designed to guarantee reasonable and continuing contact between grandparent and grandchild, based on the relationship that existed before the divorce. The law has the most clout in cases where grandparents had a full and loving relationship beforehand, according to Neil H. Stein, a family-law attorney specializing in divorce and custody cases.

Stein, who practices in Philadelphia, notes that the very existence of the law has created a positive effect; divorcing couples tend to respect the rights of their parents to see their grandchildren more now than before the legislation was enacted.

If you are experiencing this type of problem—if, for example, your son-in-law, who has custody of his children, is denying you permission to see them—the law is behind you. Don't worry about how your efforts to see your grandchildren affect your child's marriage. Nothing you do to ensure that you see your grandchildren afterward will affect the couple's marital relations. You didn't cause their stress and distress; nor will your attempts (rightfully) to see your grandchildren exacerbate it.

Also, don't be afraid to press your suit for fear of what your neighbors will think. No matter what Marge down the street or Lou at the barber thinks, you have every right to see those youngsters. The law is there to protect you and to provide family unity. Use if it you have to.

Even without resorting to legal tactics, however, there are steps in-laws and parents of divorcing couples can take to maximize their time with their grandchildren. Melissa's grandparents, Tom and Marian, had the right idea when they encouraged the teenager to call them collect. This allows a youngster to turn to grandparents as often as possible without relying on a custodial parent to foot the bill (thereby giving the parent veto power over the calls.) You should also try to be as flexible as possible in scheduling; for instance, in the case of Melissa, whose parents were battling over on whose time the trip with grandparents should occur, the grandparents could suggest that this vacation be divided, half on Jack's time, half on Sybil's.

To the bitterly squabbling parents, I urge, pull back. Now. Even if your relationship with your ex-spouse is bitter, using your child as a pawn is a dangerous tactic. At best, you will produce a youngster whose divided loyalties and anguish tear him apart; at worst, you will produce a youngster who can't wait to wash his hands of you completely when he reaches legal age. Neither option is particularly attractive.

What if you are the parents of a divorced couple—your daughter and son-in-law have split, for example—and your son-in-law, the custodial parent, has remarried? Now things become even thornier when it comes to maintaining ties with your grandchildren—but it can be done. It involves some effort to keep the lines of communication open with your ex-in-law, and it may take some heavy planning. You have to maximize opportunities for contact. Plan a lunch out with your grandchildren and your former in-law, choosing pleasant and nonthreatening surroundings. Also, invite your grandchildren to telephone anytime. In these ways, you can continue to have contact without intruding on the new marriage.

Although it might be painful to see your child's former mate remarried, continuing these visits is important, both for you and the children involved. Remember, you have a right to see your grandchildren—and your love and support for them when their parent remarries is a source of constancy in the children's lives.

The reality of divorce can create a numbers game within the family, with in-laws and former in-laws crowding the picture. Particularly if you have children whose grandparents are eager to remain close to them, you're going to face a multiplicity of mothers-in-law if you have remarried after a divorce. (And you thought handling *one* mother-in-law was a challenge!)

First and most important of all is to get off on the proper footing with the new in-laws, who may have very real concerns about your previous marital status. There is very little stigma attached to divorce these days, but your new spouse's parents may feel uncomfortable with the knowledge that you have been married before. I encourage you to be totally forthcoming in explaining that you did have a previous life, but that you have learned from that experience and that you have made a commitment to their son and have put the past behind you.

Many times, actually, getting along with your new set of in-laws is made easier by the knowledge and insight you picked up during your first marriage. You know the pitfalls of allowing boundaries to become unclear, for example; you know the dangers of unrealistic expectations and how they can wreak havoc on a relationship. So this second time around you have a foundation of knowledge to build upon. Making a mental checklist of the strengths and weaknesses of your relationship with your former in-laws can make dealing with your current ones a whole lot easier.

When the Older Couple Divorces

Fifty percent of all marriages end in divorce. More and more of those failed marriages are long term—couples who split up after twenty-five, thirty, or even forty years of struggle. Right now I'm seeing a sixty-year-old woman who has been married for thirty-five years, who has three grown children and who is in the process of calling it quits after living with her husband for more than half her life.

With these golden-year divorces comes a whole range of problems for the extended family, some similar to those experienced by younger couples, some unique. Often, the grown children are drawn into the battle, seeing one parent as aggressor, the other as victim. You have to be extremely cautious here. Maintain your neutrality about your in-laws' marriage, while bolstering your husband, who may be feeling bewildered, hurt, and betrayed by his parents' divorce. Your husband is likely to be torn, his loyalties to one parent or the other challenged.

What's your role in all of this? To listen to him, to be a sympathetic sounding board—but not to take sides. It will help you to understand what he's going through. Studies have shown that even adult children don't escape the hurt of their parents' divorce—indeed, coming at a point when the adult is in the midst of building and strengthening his own marriage, a late divorce can be even more threatening to a "child."

Whatever his emotions, you may feel that it falls to you, the daughter-in-law, to act as negotiator, as go-between. You may feel you have the responsibility of plotting family visits—and it will take all the planning that went into the invasion of Normandy to schedule who visits when. "Okay, Dad, Mother is coming for Christmas Eve, so how about if you come for Christmas dinner?" "Mom, we have Dad staying over the first two nights of Chanukah, so why don't you plan on coming the last two nights?"

In reality, holidays are for all family members, and divorce does not change this. You, the daughter-in-law, can certainly continue to invite both of your husband's parents, explaining to each that the other will be there and offering *them* the choice of whether or not to attend. Remember, they are adults; let them handle this thorny situation.

Another unexpected land mine you might encounter during your in-laws' divorce is the feeling that you have suddenly been shut out of the family. There may be more and more urgent calls between your husband and his brothers and sisters right now, as they struggle to come to grips with new and puzzling emotions. Although you may have been part of the family for ten or fifteen years, the ties that bind your husband to his siblings go back even longer, and the crisis involves the parents they have known since birth. Be patient with your husband at this point; recognize that there are times in the life cycle—most frequently times of distress, such as divorce and death—when the original nuclear family tends to come together for mutual support and comfort.

The Older Person's Responsibilities

If you are the one divorcing, one of your foremost responsibilities regarding your daughter- or son-in-law is not to drag her or him into the middle of your squabbles. Not only would that place an unfair burden on the in-law, but it could also backfire in your face. If, for example, your daughter-in-law feels her husband is being unduly hurt because of the bitterness of the divorce and your attempt to pull him into it, she may become protective of him and try to isolate him from you, perhaps by cutting down on family visits or by withholding messages to him that you have called. Then, not only will you have lost her support, you will also have lost his.

Try to keep your problems between yourselves. Don't pull other family members in; engaging children and their spouses—and *their* children—in your marital battles is destructive to the family as a whole.

When Death Closes a Chapter

I met Megan when I was invited to speak at a support group for young widows. A small-boned brunette whose thick hair was pulled back with a velvet ribbon, she told me that her husband, Ed, had recently died at age forty-three after battling lung cancer for three years. Megan was thirty-seven and was raising her seven-year-old twins, Bridgit and Kelly, virtually alone. Her in-laws, Frank and Iris Logan, had taken their son's illness and his death very, very hard, Megan said.

"While Ed was sick, they'd come to visit him in the hospital, but they couldn't stay very long—they just couldn't stand to see him so frail and in so much pain," the young woman said. Now that Ed has been gone several months, Megan and the children were trying to get their lives back together after the chaos of a devastating illness and the subsequent agony of a funeral and burial.

As she struggled to get her small family back on its feet, Megan felt very strongly that her in-laws could play a large role in keeping Ed alive in her children's hearts—and in hers. She looked to them for comfort, for continuity, and for a sense of family for Bridgit and Kelly. Then something particularly painful happened: Frank and Iris stopped calling and stopped coming over. Suddenly, the older couple dropped out of the family's lives completely, leaving Megan—vulnerable to start with—feeling bewildered, angry, and deserted.

"When I got it all together to call my mother-in-law, do you know what she told me?" Megan said. "That *she* was hurt and angry that I wasn't grieving as much as they were! She said Ed's death hurt *them* more than it hurt me! Can you believe it? And she said that one day I would get married again and forget him, but that they would never get another son."

When you've lost someone you loved very, very much, and the pain is almost unbearable, it's almost impossible to imagine that someone else can be hurting as much as you are. While this is a time when family members—including in-laws—could be pulling together, it's unfortunately also a time when the pain is so new and so raw that it's almost impossible to be considerate of others who are grieving.

At a widows and widowers' support group for people aged twenty to forty-five, sponsored by the Widow and Widows Referral Service of Philadelphia, I met more than a dozen young women and men who remember only too sadly the bitter feelings between themselves and their in-laws in the days and weeks leading up to and following their spouses' deaths. Rebecca recalled the horror of standing in the hallway of the hospital fighting with her father-in-law over who was going to tell the hospital officials where to send her husband's body. Katherine shared the story of how she and her mother-in-law fought bitterly over where Katherine's husband, Bart, would be buried after a motorcycle accident claimed his life. Marty relived the scene with his sister-in-law, Clarice, over which clergyman would officiate at services for Marty's wife, Liz—a scene that led to shouting, bitter recriminations, and ultimately the severing of relations between Marty and Clarice. This at a time when Marty desperately needed the support of close family members to see him through.

Fortunately, these sad cases are not always the rule when a loved one dies. Other participants at the support group reported that when their husbands and wives died, it was the loving presence of their in-laws that helped see them over the hard times. Jacquie, who said she'd always got along very well with her mother-in-law, said the older women went with her to choose a casket and to arrange the services for Nick—and that her warmth and strength were an inspiration for Jacquie. This was a theme I heard often: that when the relationship was good before the spouse's death, it remained good afterward, and the young widows and widowers had someone to turn to for guidance, compassion, and shared grief, yet another reason to foster good relations with your in-laws from the start.

While divorce and death both bring a relationship to an end, there is a tragic finality to death that has an even greater impact on the entire family's interactions. I call it the loss of the "connecting person"—the son/husband who provided the physical link between in-laws. When there has been a divorce, this individual is usually still around to serve this role: mother-in-law and daughter-in-law can still communicate with each other through him, if they so desire. With his death, the connection is gone—and the roles change drastically.

Now, you become "our grandchildren's mother," rather than "our daughter-in-law," and *they* become "my children's grandparents." The cement, the glue, that held you together as in-laws has disappeared, and now all of you have to work harder to keep your relationship going.

Tragically, the first time you're forced to deal with each other in these new roles is often in the immediate aftermath of the death, when emotions are screamingly raw and close to the surface. At this moment, when you're facing each other over a funeral director's desk, you have to make irrevocable decisions: Who has control over the body, who will lead the service, where will the burial be?

It's very common, at this point in the mourning cycle, when you're feeling numb and dazed with grief, to find yourself unable to make these important decisions, to feel so exhausted and drained of energy that you can't get it together to fight for what's important to you. You sit in a fog as someone else—your father-in-law, perhaps—decides that his son will be buried in the family plot and that the Reverend Cartwright, who has been the family minister for six generations, will conduct the service. Only later, when some feeling begins to creep back in, do you start experiencing regret and self-recriminations: I should have insisted that Steve be buried nearer to home; I should have insisted that he wear the blue suit he loved so much, and that we sing 'Amazing Grace,' his favorite hymn."

There are ways to prevent such regrets—and to deal with them if they surface. Here are a few suggestions for getting through this very difficult early period:

1. Invite someone who is less emotionally involved but who has your best interests in mind to accompany you to the funeral parlor—perhaps your brother or your best friend. This person

will help to clarify things for you at a time when your brain is on hold, and to settle painful differences that can arise in planning such a sad event.

2. Remember, that funerals are for the living. Whenever possible, there can be a meeting of everyone's needs. For example, if there is a dispute over which clergyperson will officiate, who says you can't have *two*? If you and your late husband followed a different religion than his parents, who not arrange to have both a Lutheran and a Unitarian minister conduct the service? You and your in-laws are already suffering enough pain; you don't need one more source of hurt and tension.
3. Take young children's needs into consideration, even over a surviving spouse's or a surviving parent's. When you're deciding where your late spouse should be buried, consider what type of trip your children will have to make to pay their respects at their parent's grave. If there are young children who will be attending the funeral, plan around their needs for a nap and for lunch, rather than those of the older mourners. If there is a conflict over religion, consider the children's feelings, and lean toward a clergyman or clergywoman who best represents the values with which they have been brought up.
4. Use a priest, rabbi, or minister to settle disputes you don't feel prepared to handle. That's their job, and they are trained to guide grieving loved ones through desperate times.
5. Keep in mind that the purpose of rituals is to help impose order or structure on situations we cannot really understand. So if a particular ritual doesn't fit into your pattern of beliefs, or if it is a source of dismay rather than of comfort, you may want to rethink its relevance for you. By the same token, if a ritual—for example, the Jewish custom of covering the mirrors in a house of mourning for seven days—*does* comfort one

party and does not offend the other, there's no harm in abiding by it. Be generous, and be flexible. There may be another ritual *you* would like to adhere to that *they* don't, and you'll want the same courtesy extended to you.

6. Finally, don't berate yourself for "giving in" to pressures to do things one way when you wanted them another way. As the initial numbness wears off and the grief starts seeping in, you may feel incredibly guilty for things you "let go"—"Damn," you castigate yourself over and over, "I should have had a closed casket. Charlie would have wanted it that way." As you work your way through the various stages of the grieving process, be aware that these details will fade after a while, and will become part of the broader picture. Let them go. You've moved beyond them at this point, and that's a healthy sign.

WHO'S GRIEVING MORE?

At the young widows' group I attended in Philadelphia, a very common theme was the competition between in-laws over who had suffered the more devastating loss. Parents often feel that the younger person can replace the dead spouse but that they have suffered an irreplaceable loss. "My mother-in-law said to me that I'd only been married to Chuck for fifteen years, but that she'd had him as a son for thirty-eight," a young bank teller told me.

In many ways, these parents are right: They *have* lost something irreplaceable. Although you know you can never replace your husband, chances are you can pick up the pieces and build a new life—even if that seems unlikely if not impossible in the days and weeks following your loved one's death. Many mental-health experts believe there is no greater devastation than the loss of a child; this is a blow from which many people never recover. So there *is* a difference in the nature of the loss, although the question of *how much* should not be a competitive match.

What if an unwinnable competition is driving a wedge between you and your in-laws? All parties have to be willing to let it go—to realize that if they hang on to the feeling that theirs was the greatest pain, they could lose not only their son or husband, but also their in-law (and perhaps their grandchildren) as well. There are several options at this point: They could sit down face to face and talk over how this (often unspoken) competition is making a painful situation even more painful; one party could write a letter to the other if a face-to-face encounter is too painful; or they could bring in a third party in the form of a more neutral family member or a social worker, whose role would be to mediate and to express objectively each person's point of view.

Once you've all taken this step, it's important to come up with a plan of action to continue building the relationship. Why continue? For the same reasons that pertain in a divorce—and then some. As painful as a divorce is for everyone involved, especially children, the pain is intensified when a death has occurred. Having a loving grandfather's arms enfold a bewildered, sobbing six-year-old can be a huge comfort in a world that suddenly feels very cold and threatening.

This type of loving support can also come from siblings-in-law. Recently, I heard a lovely story from Wilma, whose husband Alvin had died six months earlier, leaving eight-year-old Brittany and sixteen-year-old Ian feeling confused, bereft, and vulnerable. Soon after Alvin's death, his brother, Harris, began visiting the house. He engaged Ian in woodworking and gardening chores—two hobbies Harris had shared with his late brother. He took Brittany to the circus and went with Wilma to the little girl's ballet recital. "Harris filled a gap for us that otherwise would have remained open and hurting," the young widow told me. "I found it such a relief that the kids had someone they could rely on when I just had no more to give them emotionally."

Not so coincidentally, Harris was getting some rewards from filling this role, also. By working with Ian on projects Alvin had held dear, by providing a male's loving attention to Brittany, he was maintaining his connection with his brother. It was a way to keep Alvin close, even in death.

Some Hints for Bereaved Families

As I was getting ready to leave the young widows and widowers' group, I stopped to ask the participants one last question. If you could send a message to your in-laws that would help make things better between you, I wanted to know, what would you say to them?

Their answers were brief and to the point. This is the message they had for the parents of their late spouses:

1. Invite me for dinner. Include me on family outings—I'm still part of the family.
2. Call me. Reach out to me. When there's good news to be shared—my sister-in-law is expecting a baby; my brother-in-law will be graduating from high school with highest honors—please think to tell me, too. Even short phone calls make me feel connected.
3. Talk to me about my husband, your son. Use his name. Don't think that if you mention him, I'll get upset all over again. Thoughts of him are never far from my mind, anyway; being able to talk with someone who knew him so well is both a relief and a comfort. And it's a way of keeping his memory alive.
4. Allow me to show my grief in whatever way I need to: Crying, shouting, becoming withdrawn and solitary when the pain gets to be too heavy to bear. Show me *your* pain, so I will know I'm not in this alone.

Starting Over After Divorce or Widowhood

Forty-five-year-old Leila had been widowed nine years—seven years longer than her marriage to Kurt had lasted before he died of a virulent kidney infection. Her daughter, Tamara, now eleven, barely remembered her dad. Leila and her in-laws, Roy and Irma Parker, had done their best to keep his memory alive by talking of Kurt often, showing Tamara pictures of him, and sharing stories of when her father was a child.

Leila got along quite well with the Parkers. In the years since their son's death, they had gone out of their way to make the younger woman feel she was still an important member of the family. They included her in holiday celebrations, and they were available to watch Tamara while Leila studied to become a nurse. Leila had often felt that she was raising her daughter with their welcome support and guidance—and she was generous in telling them how grateful she felt.

Until Tamara was ten, the young widow was so wrapped up—first in her studies and then in her dual role as family breadwinner and family nurturer—that she barely had time to breathe, let alone consider a social life. When she finally did come up for air and realize that there was a whole world waiting for her, the Parkers were thrilled. All they wanted, Irma and Roy told each other, was for Leila to be happy.

Then Adam, a divorced business executive with three children, entered the picture. He led a seminar on financial investment a friend of Leila's convinced her to attend. The quiet emergency-room nurse and the businessman hit it off right away, and so did their children. Everyone was thrilled, including the Parkers.

Thrilled, but cautious. The older couple had some reservations, including the very real fear that Tamara—for so long as an only child and the sun, moon, and stars in her mother's universe—would feel her pivotal position threatened by the presence of three new children . . . not to mention a handsome suitor.

Problems began in earnest when Leila and Adam announced their engagement. Where once the Parkers had been cordial, even warm, toward Adam and his kids, now they were reserved. Cold. Rude at times. When the older couple came to visit, they would bring Tamara expensive toys and clothes, but nothing for the other children, not even a box of candy all three could split. They insisted on seeing Tamara alone, taking her away from the other youngsters as often as they could. They began to grill Leila: Are you going to change your name? Will Tamara change *hers*? Are you going to move away? The questions, and their tone, were out of character for Irma and Roy. Leila reacted by tensing up when they got together, and wondering where the next assault would come from.

What was really happening here? Leila's tentative first steps toward a new life were pretty threatening for her in-laws, who had invested in her all the love and caring they felt for their lost son. When the surviving spouse starts to date, all the feelings of bereavement can be dredged up again as the parents face yet one more perceived loss—that of their daughter-in-law and their grandchild. In the Parkers' minds, the upcoming marriage was both the final closing of a door and a very real threat to the lives they had woven around their daughter-in-law and their granddaughter.

When she finally came to understand the dynamics, Leila knew she had to talk with Roy and Irma. The week before the wedding, she invited them to her house, made a tasty dinner, and addressed the issue straight-on.

"I think what's going on here, Mom and Dad, is that you are missing Kurt all over again, and I can understand that. And you're afraid that when I marry Adam, I'll forget him altogether—and that Tamara will, too. But there's no way that will happen. Adam can't replace Kurt; they're two completely different people, and my life with Adam will be different than the one I had with your son.

"And I promise you, your granddaughter will never forget Kurt, either. We talk about him, how special he was, and how proud he would have been of her as she has grown. My marriage to Adam won't change that. And remember this, too: that both of you have meant a great deal to Tamara and me since Kurt died—more than you can know. I will never forget what you did for us, and how much your love sustained us. Just because I'm getting married again doesn't change that, either."

When you start to date again after you have lost your spouse, your in-laws may feel threatened, as the Parkers did. The advent of a new social life means that you are moving away from their family toward a new life. They may express their dismay in many ways, either silently or with bitter criticism: "Randall has been gone only for six months; it's not proper for you to start seeing men so soon." Or, "We don't care very much for the man you're going out with; he seems so . . . loud (quiet, fat, skinny, abrasive, retiring)," or "Don't you think little Wade will be upset if you keep seeing Malcolm?"

If your in-laws come to you with their concerns, either about the new significant other in your life or about the relative shortness of the time since your spouse died, you have a perfect right to tell them—politely—that it's your life, and that you feel at ease with the decisions you've made: "I appreciate your concern, Mother and Father Reynolds, but this is what I'm comfortable with. But that doesn't mean that I'm betraying your son (daughter). I miss him (her) also, every day."

Whether you have been widowed or divorced, remarriage demands a reworking of the existing in-law relationship, perhaps even as great a revamping as the original death or divorce necessitated. As Leila learned, your in-laws may feel very threatened. As you shift your focus onto your new marriage, they may worry—and perhaps rightly so—about being replaced in your life, about being shunted aside. They may fear that you will no longer depend on them, that the role they have played in your life is now being usurped. Somewhere deep inside, they may be terrified that once you remarry, not only is there the chance that *you* will forget their late son, but also that his memory may fade for *them*, as well.

Now is a time for patience and reassurance. You need to tell your in-laws—or your former in-laws, as you probably already refer to them—that you will never forget their child. The times you spent together as a couple—and the times they spent together as a family—will always be something you'll all carry with you.

As to the well-grounded fear that they will not be able to see you as much (and, consequently, their grandchildren) once you have remarried, that's a loss that you will all have to work out together. The reality is that if your former in-laws had got used to spending entire holidays together with you at their cabin in Maine, they may now have to settle for long weekends. In truth, they *are* experiencing a second loss, one that everyone needs to talk about and acknowledge. Yes, they will feel sad. But no, it will not help matters if they try to cling too hard, if they become nagging, confrontational, or even abusive.

What can you do if you are the older in-laws in this situation? The key is to be open to situations that will bring you together with your former daughter-in-law or son-in-law, without intruding on his or her new life. How?

1. If your son-in-law has remarried, invite his entire new family to dinners, not just him and his children. Giving the new spouse the option to decide whether or not to attend takes the pressure off your son-in-law, and will probably make him

more willing to work things out. Remember, though, that the new family is now grappling with *three* sets of parents—a thorny situation at best. Be understanding if they can't make it to dinner more than a couple of times a year.

2. Plan a meeting on an anniversary special to both you and your sister-in-law; perhaps on your late daughter's birthday. Let this be a time when just you and he and the children come together to share warm memories and to give each other some needed support at what could still be a painful time for all of you.
3. Ask to be invited to *their* family dinners; Thanksgiving, for example, is an excellent time for an extended family gathering. Don't be shy about letting the newlywed couple know that you still want to be a part of such get-togethers—remember, they can't read your mind. Don't sit in silence waiting for an invitation, thinking to yourself, "I *knew* this would happen when he got married again."
4. Understand that it's very possible the new spouse feels threatened by having you around, and that she may feel that you are a living reminder that her husband was married once before. Sound out your former son-in-law to see if this is at play here, and suggest gently and carefully that he talk with his new wife and explain that you are his children's grandparents, and it is in this role that you are visiting, not as his dead wife's parents.

Summing Up

All change is hard. After a lifetime of doing things a certain way, and interacting with family members in a particular pattern, you've suddenly lost your bearings, either through your spouse's death or through divorce. No matter how much you want to resist, this change is permanent, and you have to learn new ways. Here are some basic rules that will help you adjust:

1. Be supportive rather than judgmental. Stay neutral, rather than rushing in to be a problem-solver. Listen, offer concrete help when it's asked for, and be willing to take "no" for an answer when your suggestions aren't accepted. Realize that it's your offer that is being rejected, not *you*. The danger, when an in-law comes to you for advice, is that you immediately assume he wants you to supply immediate relief, when all he really wants is a sympathetic ear. The most productive moves you can make are to help him look at all his options and support his decision on how best to proceed from there.
2. If your daughter and son-in-law are divorcing, understand that although you feel hurt and disappointed and bewildered, the problem is basically *theirs*, not yours. If your child has died and his widow is making plans to get on with his life, realize that he is going to make decisions based on his own needs. Be respectful rather than resentful. Understand your in-laws' right to privacy, and observe the limitations they have set. Don't express anger over the actions they take or the information they choose not to share.
3. Be particularly aware that at these times of pain, tension, and stress, words often take on a life of their own. The most innocent questions—"Did you put a sweater on the baby?" "How is Zachary doing in school?"—can be misinterpreted as condemnation and accusation by a newly single parent trying to make it in a bewildering world. Realize that your words are open to more than one interpretation, and be sensitive to your in-laws' vulnerability. Of course, the single parent should not automatically interpret such statements or questions as confrontation or insult, no matter how vulnerable they're feeling. Rethink it as concern.

As children, many of us dream of being wives and mothers, husbands and fathers. Very few, if any, of us have dreams of being divorcées or widows. When we marry, we make a commitment that is supposed to last "forever." When "forever" has a limited run, when circumstances change, we have to change with them. As we change, so do our relationships with others, particularly our in-laws.

Divorce and death are at the top on any list of stress-inducers. Expecting that you will be able to adjust with a minimum amount of effort is unrealistic. This may be the most important time in your life to seek guidance and support from an impartial friend or from a counselor. As you try to reestablish balance in your life, whether you are a wife who has lost her husband or a parent who has lost a child, asking for help is a sign of strength, not a sign of weakness.

Finally, it would be helpful to realize that although circumstances have changed, through change comes growth. While it might be impossible to believe it right now, new and positive growth can come out of this experience and you may find yourself a stronger person.

CHAPTER NINE

Ten No-Fail Steps to Being a Terrible Mother-in-law

Courtship. Marriage. Parenthood. Divorce. Widowhood. Remarriage. Your in-law relationships change over the course of time, affected as much by life-cycle events and stages as by individual personalities. At the same time, some things *never* change, no matter what stage you are at in your marriage. I present Penny Bilofsky's Ten Noncommandments, or: How to be a Terrible Mother-in-law in Ten No-Fail, Easy Steps:

1. When the marriage between your child and fiancé seems inevitable, throw a temper tantrum about how you are losing your precious child. Make sure you mention how you diapered him, saw him through two weeks of chicken pox, typed his eleventh-grade history term paper—and *this* is the thanks you get.
2. After your child is married, call him at home three times a day, seven days a week. Refuse to talk with your daughter-in-law; ask only for your son.

3. Criticize your daughter-in-law's housekeeping, cooking, and parenting skills. Loudly. To anyone who will listen.
4. Criticize your daughter-in-law's parents. Compete with them to be number one in the couple's affections.
5. Nag your daughter-in-law and your son to have a baby. After all, all your friends are already grandparents, and you deserve your turn.
6. Demand details about your son and daughter-in-law's sex life. You're his mother; you have a right to know.
7. Insist that your daughter-in-law be *just like you.*
8. Never tell your daughter-in-law directly if you are hurt or angry over something. Always use your son as a go-between. That's what he's there for.
9. Demand that your son and daughter-in-law (and family) show up for dinner *at least* once a week and be present for every religious and secular holiday. Don't forget Flag Day.
10. When problems arise, always side with your son. He's perfect, isn't he?

Since I'm an equal-opportunity family therapist, I also offer: Penny Bilofsky's Ten Noncommandments for Daughters-in-law:

1. Never call your mother-in-law by any name, whether it be "Mom" or "Mother" or "Mother Miller." If you ignore her, maybe she will go away.
2. When your mother-in-law calls your home, refuse to let her talk to her son.
3. Expect your mother-in-law to keep her mouth shut and her pocketbook open. Need a new dress and the budget is stretched past the breaking point? Your mother-in-law will provide.
4. Complain to your husband about your mother-in-law constantly.
5. Complain to your mother-in-law about your husband constantly.

6. Demand that your mother-in-law take care of your kids whenever you need her. Give her no notice; she has nothing better to do.
7. Compare your mother-in-law unfavorably to your own mother. After all, there's really room for only one older woman in your life, and your own mother was there first.
8. Never acknowledge her kind gestures or thoughtful gifts. Mothers-in-law are *supposed* to do those kinds of things. Never recognize her achievements, either.
9. Exclude your mother-in-law from all the important events in your life, and withhold all information about your family life from her. It's none of her business if you're moving two thousand miles away or if you just found out that the baby you are expecting is . . . triplets.
10. Deny your mother-in-law a relationship with her grandchildren, and sabotage any bonds she begins to form with them. She has nothing good to offer them, anyway.

Are you seeing a common thread here? In the past eight chapters, we've talked about numerous issues and themes: independence versus control; reality checking versus unrealistic expectations; honesty versus lying; openness versus secrecy; setting and respecting boundaries versus crossing the lines.

We've also talked about the very strong forces that both push a mother-in-law and daughter-in-law together and pull them apart—namely, the other roles they play in the family. A daughter-in-law is also a wife and (sometimes) a mother; ditto a mother-in-law. Both are subject to the demands, real and perceived, of all those other roles. Through it all, in-laws are family, friends, peers, and strangers. Trying to balance all these roles is what makes the relationship so incredibly intense.

The Basic Skills

Although I was being just a little tongue-in-cheek back there with my "noncommandments" for in-laws, they did, in fact, contain elements of truth. As you've seen, making an in-law relationship work, really work, means becoming proficient in four basic skills that *can* be learned. These skills are:

1. Master good interpersonal communications.

   Thanksgiving was rolling around, and Thane's mother, Bea, was on the phone, asking if he and Jill would be coming for dinner this year. Thane relayed the question to Jill, who yelled back from the kitchen, "Tell your mother we're already going to my aunt Marie's house." Bea was hurt at what she saw as Jill's rejection, and Jill was annoyed that again her mother-in-law had not bothered to ask for her when she called. At no time had the two women—in-laws—spoken directly to one another.

   The episode is a study in miscommunication and missed opportunity. If Bea had taken the time to ask for Jill on the telephone, rather than talking to her through an intermediary, the older woman would have heard Jill say, "I'm delighted that you asked us, but we made these plans weeks ago. I'm really sorry, Mother Hamilton, but please ask us for Christmas." The younger woman, in turn, would have heard Bea extend her invitation directly, rather than through Thane . . . again.

   Learning to communicate directly rather than through a third party, using "I" statements that express your feelings, and looking at the person you're talking to directly in the eye rather than over her shoulder, are important ways to cement a solid relationship.

2. Set and reinforce limits and boundaries.

   Dinnertime. The kids are screaming, the dog has just overturned her water bowl on the carpet, Kathy's husband is on the phone saying he's going to be late, and, oh yeah, he's bringing his boss home for his wife's famous chicken marengo. Then the doorbell rings, and in waltzes Kathy's mother-in-law, Gloria. "I just wanted to drop by to see the kids," she chirps. "I hope it's not a bad time."

In any relationship, all parties need boundaries to guide their actions and to keep them from "overstepping" where they don't belong. Kathy, in the anecdote above, had the right—even the *obligation*—to set limits for Gloria to follow. "I enjoy your company, Mom," she might say, "but I prefer you to call before you drop by. I'd enjoy the visit much more if I weren't in the middle of a thousand things."

3. Be aware of your own expectations and learn to adjust them to the reality of the situation.

The litany was a familiar one; only the players sitting in my office had changed. Margaret spoke first: "My daughter-in-law Francine always gets annoyed when she asks me to take the kids for a weekend and I have other plans. She doesn't seem to realize that I have a full-time job and I don't always have the time—or the energy—to take care of four-year-old twins!"

Then it was Francine's turn. "I thought grandmothers couldn't get enough of their grandchildren, yet my mother-in-law doesn't seem interested in hers," she said. "I grew up spending weekends with my grandmother; she taught me how to bake and how to knit sweaters. Margaret never wants to take my girls even for a day. What a bummer."

In this scenario, Francine needed to do a little reality checking, and to realize that she was carrying around an image of a grandmother that does not apply to every woman. In her mind's eye she was seeing a gray-haired granny in an apron, standing in a kitchen elbow-deep in bread dough.

This may be someone's reality; it certainly was not Margaret's reality. Many of today's grandmothers work, ski, play tennis, run political campaigns. They love their grandchildren as much as their stay-at-home counterparts, but their lifestyles are drastically different—and so is their way of expressing love.

If Francine could adjust her expectations to reflect the real situation instead of some idealized one, she would be much happier with her mother-in-law—who, in truth, did have a very close relationship with her granddaughters.

4. Recognize core issues rather than responding to the immediate situation.

Jean had arrived for Easter dinner an hour earlier and established herself on the living room sofa. Patting the seat next to her, she said to her son, "Glen, come sit with me—I haven't seen you in so long." Just then Annette called to her husband from the kitchen, "Honey, will you come here? I need some help with the ham." Glen, torn, opted to stay with his mother; after all, she *was* the guest. Annette spent the rest of the holiday sulking that Glen hadn't "done his share" toward preparing the holiday meal as she continued to remind him bitterly throughout the day . . . and well into the next month.

What's the core issue here? Control and competition, the twin factors that play themselves out over and over in a mother-in-law/daughter-in-law relationship. Who's going to control this man—this son and husband? Who's going to "win" him ?

Understanding that this question, in one form or another, will recur at every stage of a marriage should help you recognize it when it pops up, and give you insight into the underlying struggle for the upper hand. Knowing that the struggle is there—and taking steps to defuse it—can help all parties in the relationship feel better about themselves and each other.

The Rules of the Game

Okay, you've vowed to yourself that you're going to be a good in-law—or maybe better than a good in-law, a *great* in-law. You realize it won't be easy, but you also realize that it's well worth the effort, and that the return you'll get on your investment can last the rest of your married life. Here are some rules I've drawn up to point you in the right direction. I've divided them into guidelines for parents-in-law, for daughters-in-law, and for that all-important "middle person" in the relationship, the child/spouse.

How to Be a Good Parent-in-law

1. Let your in-law make her own decision without meddling from you. Trust her good sense and maturity.
2. Try not to be critical of the people who are important to your in-law.
3. As the relationship between your child and his chosen partner deepens, expect that they will want to spend more and more time alone, together. Respect that desire.
4. Don't interfere in disagreements between your child and his spouse. If you sense trouble between them, encourage them to work it out themselves, or to get professional help if needed.
5. Be willing to contribute your ideas, and be equally willing to see those ideas rejected or redesigned.
6. Make positive comments about your child's spouse—both in private and in public.
7. Remind yourself of the nice things your in-law has done for your child, and be willing to acknowledge them aloud.

8. Understand that not all visits with your child have to include his spouse; make attempts to spend some time alone with your child.
9. If you feel "left out" of the relationship between your child and his spouse—and these feelings are perfectly normal and human—find something new to occupy yourself. Make sure that something is all yours and does not involve the children's lives (I *don't* mean getting involved in house-hunting for their new home or decorating their new living room!).
10. See your in-law as an individual; do not compare her to others, and do not become too wrapped up in the stereotype of the "perfect" in-law. That animal does not exist.
11. Praise your in-law for behaviors you like: "I enjoy it so much when you call me." "I feel good when you invite me to join you and Reid for an evening out."
12. Make your in-law feel needed.
13. Do not blame your in-law if things are not going well between you and your child.
14. Remember that you don't have to love your in-law, but you do have to respect her. A good relationship between the two of you will go a long way toward ensuring family tranquillity, solidarity, and continued contact.

How to Be a Good Daughter-in-law

1. Maintain direct contact with your in-laws; don't enlist your spouse as an unwilling "go-between." *You* invite them to dinner, buy their gifts for birthdays or Christmas, offer compliments if they look particularly nice.
2. Find a comfortable way of addressing your in-laws. Solicit their help in determining what they would like you to call them, whether it's "Mom" or "Mother Giordano," "Dad" or "Russell."

3. Try to see your in-laws as individuals separate and apart from the role they play.
4. Express interest in their interests. If your father-in-law is an antique-car buff and there's a show at the local mall, call him and see if he'd like to go with you. Mother-in-law's a Billy Joel fan? Get tickets for you and her to attend his next concert.
5. Encourage your in-laws to talk about themselves. This is a great way of understanding what they are really like.
6. Don't expect instant warmth and total bonding from the first meeting. Building a solid relationship takes time and work—on everybody's part.
7. Remind yourself that your in-law must have done something right—look at the child they raised (and *you* married).
8. Be honest with yourself about your in-laws' strengths and weaknesses. There are no perfect in-laws (or, to my knowledge, perfect people).
9. If you feel jealous about your spouse's relationship with his parents, talk to your spouse or to a good friend, so you can understand your feelings.
10. Act real and authentic with your in-laws.
11. Give your in-laws a sense that they are important in your life. Understand that a basic human emotion is the desire to be needed.
12. Recognize that you can differ with your in-law without losing the relationship—in fact, sometimes it's essential to differ in order to *maintain* the relationship. It is easier to get over hurt feelings than to get over feeling rejected by someone who is angry at you but who refuses to confront you with the issue.
13. Do not blame your in-law for any problems you are having with your spouse. The problem is between the two of you—keep it that way.

14. Prevent your in-laws from playing one person against the other (you against your spouse, for example) by maintaining open, honest communication.
15. Treat your in-laws as you would like to be treated.

How to Be a Good Child/Spouse

1. Encourage your partner and your parents to relate to one another directly. Don't allow yourself to be put in the middle.
2. Don't compare your spouse and your parents.
3. Compliment your spouse and your parents in front of each other.
4. Show respect for your spouse and your parents.
5. Never criticize your spouse to your parents; never criticize your parents to your spouse.
6. Do not tolerate criticism from either one toward the other.
7. Maintain a relationship with your parents that does not always involve your spouse.
8. Do not make your spouse responsible for the relationship between you and your parents.
9. Do not play your spouse against your parents.
10. See both your spouse and your parents in realistic terms. Remember that no one is perfect. Acknowledge that people make mistakes, but that does not make them bad. Also, acknowledge that people can change—for the better, as well as for the worse.

Eunice Winston and her two daughters-in-law were members of one family that had clearly learned the knack of getting along with each other.

The Winning Winston Way

I met them at my most recent workshop. They participated readily in the give-and-take during the presentation, then came up to me afterward, all three of them smiling. As we sipped decaffeinated coffee, the women said they just wanted me to know how fortunate they felt to have each other, and from their warmth and their ease in touching each other, I could tell they really cared.

Eunice was the mother of four sons, two of them married. She had come to the workshop because one daughter-in-law, Nina, had co-chaired the event as her social organization's closing dinner for the season. It was Nina, a social worker with a youth and family service agency, who began the conversation, her words tumbling over each other in her eagerness to describe her relationship with Eunice, her mother-in-law.

"My own mother died when I was thirteen, and I had always longed for a close relationship with an older woman. When I met Dwight, Eunice's openness and her receptiveness toward me made my feelings about Dwight even stronger. Now, we've been married five years, and I have to tell you that I have the world's best mother-in-law." Nina stopped and put her arm around Eunice. "She never intrudes, she never pries about Dwight's and my business, but she's always there if we need her, and she has encouraged me in every step of my career."

Theresa, the other daughter-in-law, took up the story, leaning over the table as she described her own experience. "I've been married to Ted for eleven years, and we have three great kids. I value Eunice because she gives me the space I need. I know she adores the children, and she's always eager to see them, but I know that I always have the privilege to say 'No, today's not good for us,' and she won't be hurt or offended. That makes it so much easier, and pleasant, to say yes whenever I can.

"Another thing," Theresa went on. "My own mother lives nearby, and Eunice never resents the time I spend with her. She never tries to compete for my attention, and that means a lot to me. When I had bronchial pneumonia last year, my mother came over every day to take care of me. I knew Eunice was concerned; she offered her help and her support, but she kind of held back out of respect for my mom. How many women would do that?"

Through both recitations, Eunice, a tall woman with mahogany-colored hair twisted in a braided coil, had listened with a delighted smile on her face. I couldn't resist the opportunity, so I asked her, "Tell me, what's your secret? What are you doing right?" She was silent for a few moments before she started speaking, slowly, as if she were deep in thought.

"There really is no secret, except for the fact that I see each of my daughters-in-law as an individual and try to treat her that way. I never compare them with each other, and I respect them for their differences.

"As the mother of four sons, I was really looking forward to expanding my family when they married. I always trusted my relationship with my boys, and I had every confidence that the women they brought home would fit in.

"I guess if there *were* a secret to my success, it would be that I respect Nina and Theresa as *people*, and I act accordingly. I would no sooner drop in on one of them unannounced than I would a close friend. Even if I were in the neighborhood, I'd call first. And if they said they were busy, I would understand that they have lives of their own, and not take it as rejection."

Eunice stopped, then pulled each of the younger women close in an embrace. "It works both ways, you know—I get an awful lot back from these two ladies. Although I know they're both very busy every day—Nina with her job, Theresa with the children—they never exclude me. They let me know that they value my opinions, and even though they don't do things the way I do, they never make me feel like a old fogy. They listen, and that's what makes me feel important to them.

"And most of all," Eunice said with a grin, "they make my sons happy."

All three finished talking, and I realized once again that maybe not *all* but most in-law relationships have the potential to be like this: warm, caring, respectful. A bond like this doesn't just *happen*, and it's more than just potluck. It takes work, commitment, a sense of humor, some real honesty, and mutual respect. But as the three smiling women at my table could attest, it's worth it. It's very worth it.

ABOUT THE AUTHORS

PENNY BILOFSKY M.S.S., L.S.W., is a psychotherapist in private practice in Cherry Hill, N.J., and Philadelphia. She received her bachelor's degree from Rutgers University and her master's in social science from Bryn Mawr College. She is a lecturer at the School of Social Work, Rutgers University, and the University of the Arts, Philadelphia.

A board-certified diplomate of clinical social work, she has had many years of experience counseling people with personal, marital, family, and work-related problems. Ms. Bilofsky has led workshops and seminars around the country on in-law relations, and has appeared on radio and television talk shows. She has also written newspaper columns describing life cycle events and their impact on the family.

She and her husband, Allan, who live in New Jersey, have two daughters.

FREDDA SACHAROW is associate editor of the Jewish Exponent

of Philadelphia and a freelance writer whose work appears frequently in the *New York Times* and in *Inside* magazine. She was formerly a staff writer for the *Philadelphia Bulletin* and for the *Burlington County Times*. Ms. Sacharow has won numerous national writing awards, including the Boris Smolar Award for Excellence in North American Jewish Journalism.

She and her husband, Steven, live in New Jersey with their daughter.